Creative SERGING

THE COMPLETE HANDBOOK FOR DECORATIVE OVERLOCK SEWING

Revised Third Edition

by
Pati Palmer
Gail Brown and
Sue Green

Book Design & Production by
Wisner Associates, Portland, Oregon

Technical and Fashion Illustrations
by Kate Pryka

Divider Page Fashion Illustrations
by Maggie Raguse

Third Edition Editor by Marta Alto

PALMER/PLETSCH PUBLISHING

We could not have written this book without the gracious cooperation of many sewing machine companies that manufacture and/or distribute sergers. Our special thanks are extended to the following firms, listed in alphabetical order: Babylock USA (babylock.com), Bernina of America (berninausa.com), Brother International (brother.com), Elna USA (elnausa.com), Euro-Pro (sharkcompany.com or through the retail outlet site), Janome America (janome.com), Kenmore (sears.com), Juki Company (juki.com), Necchi (allynint.com), Pfaff American Sales Corp. (pfaffusa.com), Simplicity (simplicitysewing.com), Riccar America (riccar.com), Singer Company (singerco.com), Toyota (toyotasewingmachines.com), Viking Sewing Machines (husqvarnaviking.com), White (whitesewing.com). Please note that serger model names may differ from the company names, and that some companies offer several different serger lines. Visit the web sites listed here for more information and dealer referrals. We encourage you to shop at your local sewing machine dealership, where you will find a range of models and prices, knowledgeable salespeople, how-to classes, machine parts and repair services.

In addition, we would like to thank Coats & Clark Inc., Swiss Metrosene, Inc., Y.L.I. Corp., McCall Pattern Company; Marta Alto, Naomi Baker, Lynette Ranney Black, Karen Dillon, Ann Price, Susan Pletsch, Lynn Raasch, Barbara Weiland, and Leslie Wood of Palmer/Pletsch Associates; and Bobbie Keeney, who remains our most proficient typist. Also, we thank Thelma Watson and Hazel Jens, avid home sewers who read our book for clarity; Ron Ellwanger, Jeff Watson, and Jack Watson, for putting up with us through the writing of this book. And to Pati's patient new daughter, Melissa, born during the writing of this book!

ABOUT THE AUTHORS

For thirty years, Gail Brown has been writing about how to sew, serge and decorate better—and faster. Her 14 books include one of the industry's all-time bestsellers: Sewing with Sergers, written with Pati Palmer (see page 128) and her latest release, Simply Napkins. She is internationally recognized for her many television and video appearances on Sewing with Nancy (PBS), Sew Perfect (HGTV) and Our Home (Viacom/Lifetime). From Gail's home office in Hoquiam, WA, she designs head covers for hair-loss sufferers, and continues to write for Sew News (the "Giving Back" column), the Creative Kindness website creativekindness.com) and her own web site (gailbrown.com). Sewing—and teaching friends and family to sew—remain her favorite pastimes.

Pati Palmer owns her own publishing company, designs "Personalized Instruction" patterns for the McCall Pattern Company, and speaks to audiences throughout the U.S. and Canada sharing her extensive knowledge. In her career she has worked as an educational representative for the Armo Company, as Corporate Home Economist for an Oregon department store, and as a notions buyer. She is a Home Economics graduate in Clothing and Textiles from Oregon State University and was recently selected Oregon Home Economist of the Year. She has been Vice Chairman of the Clothing and Textiles section of the American Home Economics Association and National Public Relations Chairman for Home Economists in Business. Pati writes for *Sew News* and *McCall's Pattern Magazine*. She has co-authored *Mother Pletsch's Painless Sewing* (newly revised), *Pants for Any Body, Sewing Skinner® Ultrasuede® Fabric, Easy, Easier, Easiest Tailoring,* and *Sewing With Sergers.* Pati and Gail have both appeared on the Sewing by Satellite national teleconference.

Sue Green was a serger pioneer, one of the first to travel and teach serger techniques. She entertains audiences with her light-hearted approach to this technical subject, not to mention that she can single-handedly take apart and reassemble any serger! As former sewing machine and serger sales manager for a large fabric store chain, Sue was responsible for designing "how-to" lesson programs. As National Education Coordinator for one of the largest serger importers, she traveled the country conducting dealer training and consumer programs. She also developed serger workbooks and revised manuals. Sue continues to teach and write. Her newest book is *Threads, Threads, and More Threads.*

3

TABLE OF CONTENTS

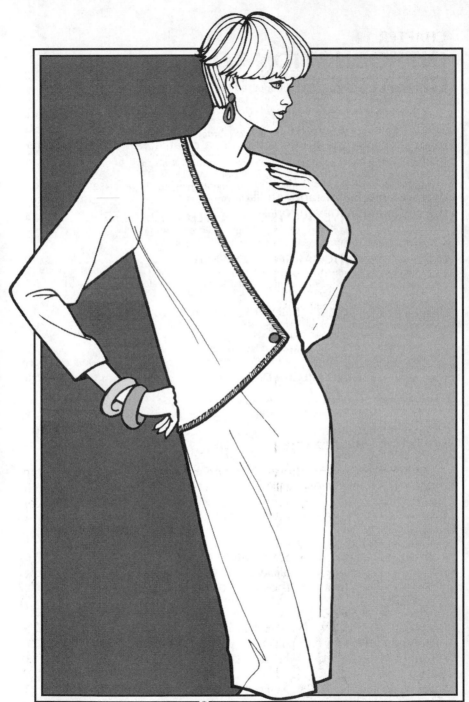

INTRODUCTION TO *Creative Serging*

CHAPTER 1

INTRODUCTION TO CREATIVE SERGING

Creativity means originality, expressiveness and imagination. Sergers give us decorative possibilities that open a whole new world of creativity for the home sewer . . . a creativity that looks sophisticated, not cutesy!

A serger trims, then totally encases an edge of fabric unlike the zigzag on a conventional sewing machine. Also, since the stitches are formed over a metal stitch finger, the edge will never draw up, even on lightweight silkies. Because sergers have "loopers" that go **over** and **under** the fabric, heavy decorative threads, yarns, and ribbons can be used. These cannot be used on conventional machines because they will neither fit through the needle nor penetrate many fabrics.

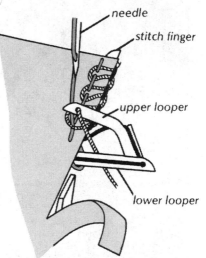

WHAT IS DECORATIVE SERGING?

Whenever serging shows, it is decorative . . . even when using regular thread. Serging will show **more** if you shorten the stitch length, use a contrasting color thread, a heavier thread, or a shinier thread like silk, rayon, or metallic. The following are decorative uses of a serger:

- Exposed seams
- Satin stitched seam allowances that look like they are bound

- Edges finished with a wide stitch

- Rolled edges serged with matching or contrasting thread

- Flatlocked seams

- Heirloom sewing with laces and trims attached with serging

Our first book, **Sewing With Sergers** (see page 128), covered serger basics. Since then, we've learned a lot more about the use of decorative threads and creative uses of a serger. We will help you be adventurous and experiment with many different ideas. Also, we can now help you **solve** nearly **every problem** you might encounter on your serger. Thanks to our four-day Palmer/Pletsch Serger Workshops held in Portland, Oregon, we've learned a **lot**!

SERGERS HAVE IMPROVED

During the last 30 years, millions of sergers have been manufactured in Japan and Taiwan and sold to home sewers in this country. The growth curve has been steep—in 1976, only 20,000 sergers were imported into the U.S. compared to 600,000 in 1986. In fact, it is estimated that today, nearly one out of every four home-sewing households also owns a serger. With this increase in sales, has come technological improvements and many new features: built-in lights, external dials for adjusting stitch width and length, easier threading (including pneumatic as on the Baby Lock) and tension adjusting, differential-feed capability, new stitch formations (such as the coverstitch), improved instruction books and videos, and now even computerized stitch-selection panels. All of these contribute to our ability to use sergers creatively.

If you already own a serger, keep your first one even if you decide to upgrade. Today's luxury is having TWO sergers, like TWO cars! Keep one set up for regular seaming and one for rolled edge or flatlocking—or one always with white thread.

MAKE YOUR FIRST DECORATIVE PROJECT EASY

For your first creative venture, choose one of the lighter weight decorative threads such as topstitching thread or Woolly Nylon and an easy-to-sew inexpensive fabric such as polar fleece or sweatshirting. For ideas, see our chapter on decorative sweatshirts.

The most important guideline for decorative serging is to **TEST** using a scrap of your garment fabric on the same grain. By adjusting the tension dials just a little, you can totally change the stitch or create a new one.

Child's decorative polar fleece coat

A creative sweatshirt

Once you've mastered decorative serging basics, graduate to heavier threads, yarns, and ribbons. Use this book to hold your hand as you become ULTRA CREATIVE. You won't believe how much fun you will have!

CHAPTER 2
SERGER BASICS

The serger, also called an overlock machine, stitches, trims, and overcasts in one step at almost twice the speed of a conventional sewing machine. A conventional sewing machine sews from 700 to 1100 stitches per minute and a serger sews up to 1700 stitches per minute.

Note: It is easier to understand what tension dials do when they can be seen mounted on the front of the machine. Most sergers today have tension dials that are set into the machine.

needle

stitch finger

upper looper

knife

lower looper

"George"

THE PARTS OF A SERGER

One important part of a serger is not illustrated in our first book is what Sue lovingly calls "George." George is the extension on the back of the presser foot. Always put your threads under George before beginning to serge!

A 5-thread serger is illustrated here so that you can see the parts of a machine that has the maximum number of loopers and needles. For a 4-thread machine, just eliminate the left lower looper. For a 3-thread machine eliminate one needle as well.

telescoping thread guide

spool rod

needle thread tensions

upper looper tension

lower looper tension

needles

presser foot

upper knife

lower knife

upper looper

fly wheel

left lower looper

right lower looper

suction cups

A machine that also does a cover stitch has extra needles. Most of the cover stitch sergers are computer aided.

HOW ARE STITCHES FORMED ON SERGERS?

The Stitch and Stitch Formation

PLAY CATCH METHOD: You unthread and plug the upper looper, turning it into a "V"-shaped "hook." The lower looper goes under the fabric and hands a loop of thread to the upper looper which then places it on top of the fabric ready to be caught by the needle. This method is used on machines that do 3-thread stitches where the upper looper goes back and forth over the top of the fabric only and cannot go over AND under the fabric.

3-Thread Overlock—The threads connect or "lock at the seam line, and the stitch looks approximately the same on both sides.

The upper looper goes *over* the top of the fabric leaving a loop which is caught by the needle.

The lower looper goes *under* the fabric placing a loop of thread under the needle loop then goes out to the edge where it knits together with the upper looper thread.

3/4-Thread Overlock—
A 3-thread stitch with an extra needle thread.

All 3/4-thread machines will make a 3-thread stitch alone. Simply eliminate a needle. Some machines have a width control dial that gives some adjustment to the finished stitch.

Stitch Characteristics and Uses

- Called an "overedge" stitch because the threads do not connect or "lock" at the seamline; therefore, it is not used to sew seams.

NOTE: One manufacturer has invented the term "**seamlock**" for a 2-thread **seam**. They feel a strong seam can be sewn by tightening the needle tension all the way and loosening the looper tension. The needle thread then forms a straight line and the looper wraps the edge.

- Perfect if you primarily want to finish seam allowances and edges.
- With only two threads, seam and edge finishes are less bulky — nice for lightweight fabrics or when using heavier decorative threads.
- Flatlocking is easy and stronger with a 2-thread stitch. (See page 52.)
- A 2-thread balanced stitch can be adjusted to a rolled edge.

- Called an "overlock" stitch because the threads connect or "lock" at the seamline. Can be used to sew seams.
- Produces a balanced stitch that looks similar on both sides...great for reversibles.
- With three threads, seam and edge finishes can be slightly bulkier than with two threads because of the additional thread.
- Has lots of give, so is excellent for knits.
- 3-thread machines can flatlock (see page 52).

NOTE: Some 3-thread machines can convert to two threads. Check your manual.

- Can be adjusted to sew a rolled edge.
- Ideal for decorative edges with either left or right needle.

- Like a 3-thread stitch with the addition of an extra stitch down the middle for added durability.
- May serge with only three threads.
- Has as much give as a 3-thread stitch.
- Interesting decorative effects created when different color threads are used in the needles. 3/4-thread machines can flatlock, but one needle must be dropped.
- Use both needles to seam wovens.
- Using both needles with differential feed produces better gathers.

NOTE: Several manufacturers have 3/4-thread machines that can also sew a 3-thread as well as a 2-thread stitch. We call them 2/3/4-thread machines.

13

5-Thread Stitch—A chain combined with a 3-thread overlock:

The chain—the left needle and left lower looper form a 2-thread chain stitch.

The 3-thread overlock—formed as described on page 12.

Conversion option: The 3-thread overlock on many 5-thread machines can be converted to a 2-thread overedge. This is a 4-thread but with a chain and 2-thread overedge.

The chain—formed as described above.

The 2-thread overedge—formed using the play catch method described on page 12.

Cover Stitch—2 or 3 needles and one under looper, which is generally not the same one as the lower looper.

Two to three needle positions determine how many needles and the width between stitches.

5-7.5mm wide   2.5mm wide   5-7.5mm wide

- Sews a 2-thread chain stitch in combination with a 2-thread overedge or a 3-thread overlock stitch.
- Chain stitch, 2-thread overedge, or 3-thread overlock can each be used independently.
- By using the 2-thread chain stitch **and** 3-thread overlock stitch together, the seam is sewn twice for added durability.
- Use the 3-thread overlock stitch alone for seams that require stretch.
- Can sew rolled edges with either 2-thread or 3-thread stitch.
- A very wide 9mm seam width created on some machines when the chain is sewn with either the 2- or 3-thread stitch. Great for durability!!

- Cover hem — decorative topstitch and finish at once.
- Attach elastic.
- Chain stitch for basting or decorative work.
- Cover stitch for perfect belt loops

CHAPTER 3

Decorative Thread

GLOSSARY

DECORATIVE THREAD GLOSSARY

Use this chapter as a reference when choosing and serging with decorative threads, yarns, and ribbons. We've listed them in order of serging difficulty starting with the easiest. At the end of the chapter we've summarized tension tips for each type in a handy quick-reference chart.

Regular Thread — Choose extra-fine, serger, or all-purpose thread. The latter is the heaviest, yet the difference is subtle. One advantage of using any of these threads decoratively is that you can use them in the needle as well as the loopers. Also, all-purpose thread is available in a wide range of colors.

For better coverage, we recommend a short stitch length when using regular thread, especially on the edge of a woven fabric. We call a short stitch a "satin" stitch. With knits or non-wovens you can use a longer stitch length if a more open look is desired.

For conventional spools, use the cap that comes with your machine to help the thread reel off quickly and evenly. Place the cap on the spool or the rod. Check your manual. Place the notched side of the spool down.

notch

Creative Uses:

- Lapped seams and edges on a shirt
- Lightweight rolled edges on a scarf or full skirt hem
- Serged seams exposed on the right side

Nylon Filament Thread — Some ready-to-wear manufacturers use this translucent thread in their general sewing so they don't need to change thread every time they change fabric color. It automatically "matches" the fabric. Most of the newer nylon thread is soft and not wirey. It can used in the needle as well as in both loopers. Tension settings are generally normal. You may need to cover the spool with netting to prevent spilling or slipping off the spool.

Fold the net down so it doesn't catch on the thread as it spools off.

17

One of our favorite uses of nylon filament thread is in the needle and the lower looper. Use a heavy decorative thread, yarn or ribbon in the upper looper. The "invisible" nylon makes the upper looper thread appear as if it is just floating on the surface of the fabric.

NOTE: A semi-transparent polyester thread is also available and comes in several colors. Also, high-sheen acrylic topstitching threads, serge smoothly and trouble-free, too.

Topstitching Thread—A highly twisted, cord-like polyester or cotton-covered polyester thread in a buttonhole twist. It covers an edge better than regular thread and is available in many colors.

Topstitching thread can be used in the needles as well as the loopers. Use a large spool cap because the thread tends to embed itself on the spool. The wide angle created by the spool cap (page 17) helps the thread flow freely.

We love topstitching thread (also known as "buttonhole twist") and some manufacturers are now putting more than 50 yards on a spool: Jeans Stitch by YLI, and Sulky 12 weight. Before beginning, make sure you have enough thread to complete an entire edge. See page 27 for estimating yardage. Test first, but if you do run short, see page 35. For shorter yardage projects, 50-yard Coats Dual Duty Plus works well. We suggest buying one spool **just for testing.**

Creative Uses:

- Flatlocked and fringed challis scarves
- Edges of coats and jackets that are serged rather than stitched and turned
- Wonderful for rolled edges on napkins as it washes well
- Decorative stitching on synthetic suedes and leathers
- Flatlocking on sweatshirts and actionwear (washes well)

Rayon Thread — Looks similar to silk with its beautiful sheen, but much less costly. Available in fine, medium, and heavy weights, the most prevalent is a weight about halfway between regular and topstitching thread.

Rayon thread is primarily used in the upper looper. It tends to break easily when used in the needle and lower looper due to friction. It also slips through the tension discs easily due to its slickness, so you may need to tighten the tensions slightly. Serge a test sample. For rolled edges use it only in the upper looper. The lower loop needs to be tightened a lot, difficult with thin slippery thread. It is available on cones and spools and may need netting to keep it from spilling.

Rayon thread comes in a wide range of very intense colors including variegated. It also comes in heavier weights. Brands include Madeira, Sulky, Y.L.I., Robinson Anton, and Coats & Clark.

Creative Uses:

- Wide, shiny satin stitch on the edge of Chanel-style jackets (resembles trim.) Use a heavier rayon thread like Decor 6, Designer 6 or Crown Pearl Rayon in a satin stitch on the edge of a Chanel-style jacket to resemble trim.

- Rolled edges on scarves
- Medium width satin stitch in unlined jackets to resemble a silky Hong Kong seam finish
- Shiny rolled edge seams in heirloom sewing

NOTE: There are shiny polyester threads available as well.

Silk Thread—Both Things Japanese and Y.L.I. sell imported silk threads in a range of weights It is similar in look and stitching characteristics to rayon, but with a color and sheen unique only to silk.

Woolly Nylon — In 1984, Y.L.I. introduced their Woolly Nylon to the homesewing market. It is a heat-set texturized or crimped thread that looks fuzzy like wool. It is about the same weight as regular sewing thread; however, because it is lofty and not twisted, it spreads to cover an edge. A similar product is Metroflock by Metrosene.

These threads can be used in the needle as well as the loopers. We find it necessary to loosen tensions considerably to allow it to flow without too much stretching. The inherent stretchiness actually "tightens up" the seam making a **very strong** seam that won't pull apart — perfect for activewear.

Creative Uses:

- Rolled edges for napkins, or any narrow hem.
- Edges of placemats — good "coverage", washable, and prevents corners from ravelling
- Seams in ravelly fabrics or activewear when strength is essential

Metallic Thread — There is a difference among brands. Some are very fine, resembling silk, while others are coarse and metal-like. Your choice depends on the look you want. Metallics work best in the upper looper. Some will strip back or fray when used in the needle or lower looper. Test first!

Use a matching color non-metallic thread in the needle to blend with the metallic thread in the looper. With a shorter stitch length, the coarser metallics lie at random. They don't look as smooth and even as the finer metallics. Try tightening the tensions slightly to smooth them out. Some may look better with a longer stitch length. They come on cones, tubes and spools.

Creative Uses:

- Rolled edges on holiday napkins
- A wide satin stitch on edges of placemats
- Pin tucks on an evening blouse
- Ruffles on sheers
- Dancewear
- Fancy scarf edges
- Dramatic touch on a basic black or white dress

Crochet Thread — Available in cotton or acrylic fibers and in many colors. The cotton variety, a highly twisted mercerized thread, is slightly thicker than topstitching thread. It is strong and easy to use in upper as well as lower loopers, but too thick for the needle. The acrylic variety is similar to cotton only slightly fuzzier, hence a perfect coordinate for wools and sweater knits. Coats & Clark is a major manufacturer of these and their Knit-Cro-Sheen is available in both cotton and acrylic. Crochet thread is wound on balls that average 175 yards each. See pages 27 and 32 for hand feeding and tension tips.

Creative uses:

- Gail sewed a single-layer jacket without facings using upholstery fabric. She used crochet thread in both loopers to finish the outside edges, making the jacket reversible.
- Edges of quilted placemats.
- Edges of thick fuzzy woolens to create your own blankets and throws.

Pearl Cotton—A mercerized 100% cotton that is shiny, soft, and not highly twisted. Two widely distributed sizes are #8 (finer) and #5 (thicker). It is available in 50 or 100 yard balls or smaller 25 yard skeins. Its color range is broad and includes interesting variegated shades.

Our preference is to use pearl cotton in the upper looper. You can use it in the lower looper, but the extra thread guides can cause fraying. Also, because of the loose twist, the needle can catch the pearl cotton as it is "thrown" over the top of the fabric by the upper looper. Serging slowly will generally solve this problem. See page 27 and 32 for hand feeding and tension tips. It is best to wind it onto a cone for easiest serging.

Creative Uses:

- Flatlocked fringe on a wool challis scarf

- Edges of a cotton interlock knit in a sporty jumpsuit using a bright contrast color

- Edges of baby clothes and receiving blankets using a variegated pastel color
- Placemats as it washes well

Yarn — The key to successfully serging with yarn is to use one that is fine, strong, tightly twisted, and smooth. To test for adequate strength, pull on a strand. If it breaks easily, it will also break easily when serging. If too loosely twisted, it can be caught by the needle and jam your machine. If lumpy, it won't flow evenly through the tension guides.

Easy to use—a fine baby yarn or knitting machine yarn that is tightly twisted and even.

Do not use—a thick slubby untwisted yarn.

We've had good luck with baby yarn (comes in pastel and variegated shades), as well as sock or sweater yarn (comes in neutral colors). Both are fine, strong and twisted enough for smooth feeding. Sport or "fingering" weight yarns are available in a wider color range, but each brand and fiber varies, so test serge on scraps **first**.

Keep fiber content in mind too. Acrylic yarn works well as it is quite strong. Wool yarn is weaker, but twisting the plies can add strength. Blending wool with nylon also helps. New yarn-look threads for machine embroidery work well.

Yarn is generally used in the upper looper only. The extra thread guides in the lower looper can cause fraying. See pages 27 and 32 for feeding and tension tips.

Creative Ideas

- Variegated pastel yarn on edges of a double-layer receiving blanket

- Edges of a single-layer wool or fleece cape

- Edges of a boiled wool or fleece jacket

- Neckline, sleeve and hems of a sweater or fleece top

Ribbon — Soft knitting ribbon 1/6" to 1/4" wide works well in the upper looper of a three-thread and the looper of a two-thread serger. See pages 27 and 32 for feeding and tension tips. Y.L.I. is one of the major distributors of decorative knitting ribbons. The following are available.

Silk Ribbon — Expensive, but can be purchased by the yard, rather than by the spool. See page ___ for estimating yard

Acrylic Ribbon — Very shiny, drapable, and soft like silk, but less expensive. Often called synthetic silk. Another suitable silk substitute is rayon, but may, however, break more than the acrylic silk-likes.

Cotton Ribbon — Durable and washable. Great as a trim for children's clothes. Choose a very fine, soft type for easiest sewing.

Polyester Ribbon — Generally too stiff, but worth a test.

Creative Ideas:

- Edges of ruffles for childrenswear and frou-frou blouses
- Edges of sweaterknits . . . the combination of textures is lovely
- As part of an heirloom serging scheme, add a row or two of ribbon serging

DECORATIVE THREAD, YARN, AND RIBBON GUIDE

The next chapter goes into detail on handling decorative thread, yarn, and ribbon; however, use this handy chart for quick reference.

Thread	Needle(s)	Upper Looper	Lower Looper	Tension
Clear Nylon	Yes	Yes	Yes	Normal
Topstitching	Yes	Yes	Yes	Slightly Looser
Rayon	Can Break	Yes	Can Break	Tighten
Woolly Nylon	Yes	Yes	Yes	Loosen
Metallic	May Fray	Yes	May Fray	Normal, Test
Crochet	Too Thick	Yes	Sometimes	Loosen a Lot
Pearl Cotton	Too Thick	Yes	Sometimes	May need to loosen or remove completely from tension disc and/or thread guides.
Yarn	Too Thick	Yes	Sometimes	
Ribbon (silky)	Too Thick	Yes	Sometimes	

Decorative Basics

CHAPTER 4

DECORATIVE BASICS

Read this chapter before you begin decorative serging and you will avoid lots of frustration. Decorative serging is very creative, but you are pushing your serger to do more than its basic functions. With patience, you will be able to create looks you've never before thought possible. You'll really have a one-of-a-kind garment!

WHERE TO USE DECORATIVE THREADS ON YOUR SERGER

Generally, we use heavier decorative threads in the **upper looper**. There are fewer thread guides, so less stress is exerted on the thread. The lower looper has two holes and more thread guides causing stress and thread breakage.

Lighter weight decorative threads can be used anywhere, even in the needle. Make sure the needle is large enough to accommodate the thread, yet not so large it damages the fabric. We use a size 14 for topstitching thread and an 11 or 12 for regular thread.

NOTE: Today's sergers generally use a standard sewing machine needle. The "metallic" needle has a larger eye, great for some heavier threads.

THREADING TIPS

- **Thread in proper order** — Check your manual for recommended order. In our first book we started with the lower looper, but since the upper looper thread guides are usually **behind** the lower looper thread guides, it may be easier to begin with the upper looper, then thread the lower looper and finally the needle.

- **All guides must be threaded!** — Missing a guide is the number one cause of stitching problems on a serger! Always DOUBLECHECK the guides!

- **Make sure the looper threads aren't tangled or they will break!**

Good!
Totally
separate

Good!
Lower looper thread
over upper looper
thread

Disaster!
Lower looper thread
between upper
looper and upper
looper thread

- **Don't use too heavy thread, yarn, or ribbon** — As a rule of thumb, if you have to **force** a double layer of decorative thread through the looper, it is **too** heavy to use on your machine.

- **There is an easy way to get a heavy thread through a small hole** — You can bend or break the looper threader that comes with some machines if you use it with heavy threads.

Instead, form a thread "cradle".
Cut twelve inches of regular
thread and wrap it around
your heavier thread forming a
loop. Then thread **both** ends
of the regular thread through
the looper hole. Use tweezers
if necessary. Pull the heavier
thread through the hole.

- **Be sure threads are engaged in tension discs** — Tug on threads just above and below the tension discs to make sure they are engaged. You should feel resistance on each thread.

- **After threading, "clear" threads before beginning to stitch** —

If you turn the flywheel
around while threading, the
needle thread will wrap
around the lower looper causing breakage.

To prevent this problem, slide
a seam ripper or similar tool
under presser foot to draw up
needle thread.

HOW MUCH DECORATIVE THREAD WILL I NEED?

It is frustrating to run out of thread. To estimate what is needed, Sue serged one yard of fabric with five types of decorative threads, yarns, and ribbons. Then she measured the amount used. Her stitch length was 2.5mm and width 5.0mm. She found the following:

Thread	Yards per looper needed to sew one yard of fabric
Pearl cotton	6-1/2
Topstitching thread	7
Crochet thread	8
Sport yarn	5-1/2
1/8" ribbon	7-1/2

Add to these amounts one yard for threading the machine and at least six yards for testing. Of course, if you change your stitch length and width, the amounts given in the chart will vary.

You may wonder why more crochet thread is used than ribbon. Crochet thread is wiry and lies on the fabric in a neat rounded "S" pattern. Ribbon is softer and folds over on top of itself; therefore, less is used. Why is so much less yarn used? Yarn stretches or elongates as it goes through the machine.

REEL OFF BY HAND WHEN USING SKEINS OR BALLS

If your decorative thread, yarn, or ribbon is **not** wound on spools, you must make sure it **feeds freely** as you serge. Any restriction on the thread will cause uneven stitching.

Hand winding pearl cotton or yarn onto an empty cone is the easiest way to use these heavier threads. However, you can also place the ball or skein on its side on the table next tot he machine, in a bowl, or on the floor. Then reel off a large quantity and serge—reel and serge—reel and serge. Just don't forget to keep reeling so there is plenty of slack between the ball or skein and the first thread guide.

ALWAYS TEST FIRST!

It's difficult to correct a mistake. Pati learned the hard way. Her round-neck top grew into a "U"-neck style, because she forgot to test. After all, the **easiest** way to correct a problem is to cut away your mistake!!

You will need 30" of fabric for thorough testing. Test on the same grain you'll be sewing. A **long** strip of fabric allows you to serge 5", stop and look at both sides, adjust tensions if necessary, and serge another 5". Do this until you achieve the look desired.

SEW SLOWLY!

We can't emphasize enough the importance of sewing **slowly**. Even though your serger was made for speed, heavier threads pose a variety of potential problems. Also, if you serge too fast, extra tension will be placed on the thread and cause uneven stitching.

STITCH WIDTH

A wider stitch shows off the decorative thread better. We recommend beginning your TEST sample with the widest stitch and narrowing it a little at a time until you achieve the look you want.

STITCH LENGTH

Begin serging your TEST sample with the **longest** stitch possible to prevent jamming under the presser foot. Gradually work shorter until the desired look is achieved. Remember, "fatter" threads take up more room (as shown in our example) even though the stitch length is the same.

"Thin" thread   "Fat" thread

STEPS TO HEADACHE-FREE DECORATIVE SERGING

After threading the machine, use the following order for TEST sewing:

1. Set the stitch length and width according to the above instructions.

2. Rotate the handwheel by hand. See if the stitches are forming on the stitch finger.

3. It is not always necessary to lift presser foot during regular serging. However, you MUST LIFT the presser foot and place fabric under it when using decorative threads. It helps begin the "feeding" and prevents jamming.

4. Always at least **skim** the fabric edge with the knives for even width stitches, even if not trimming away any seam allowance.

5. Begin sewing SLOWLY! Check your stitches every five inches.

YOUR THREAD BREAKS DURING TESTING

If one of your threads breaks during testing, try the following:

1. Double-check to see if the machine is threaded correctly.

2. Check to see if the threads are caught in the spool's notch.

3. Check to see if all threads are engaged in tension discs.

4. Try loosening the tension on the thread that broke.

5. If all else fails, re-thread the machine from scratch!

6. It still breaks? Re-thread the machine with regular thread in order to determine whether you have a mechanical problem or your machine just doesn't like that particular decorative thread.

EVERYTHING YOU EVER WANTED TO KNOW ABOUT TENSION

Most sergers have tension dials. Sue prefers not to use this term. It reminds her of tension headaches! Instead, she calls them "stitch formers." And, that is really what they are. Even a slight tension change can alter the look of a stitch. In decorative serging, there is no RIGHT or WRONG tension—whatever tension achieves the look is the correct tension.

NOTE: See our first book, **Sewing With Sergers**, for in-depth tension diagrams for all types of stitches.

Tension dials are mounted either on the outside or set into the machine. The dials are numbered for loosening or tightening. If front mounted, we say "RIGHTY, TIGHTY, and LEFTY, LOOSEY." Silly as it sounds, you won't forget. If they are built in, up loosens and down tightens or usually the larger number, the tighter the tension. Computerized sergers that control the tension have some override capacity. Then, there is a serger brand that does not have tension dials, but a thread feeding system that works well.

WHICH DIAL CONTROLS WHICH THREAD?

Usually, the two on the left control the needles and the two on the right control the loopers with the furthest right controlling the lower looper. Mark them with masking tape until you can quickly remember their function.

left   right   upper   lower
needle needle   looper   looper

NOTE: Most of today's serger have built-in tension dials rather than front mounted as in our illustration.

THE SECRET TO CORRECTING TENSION PROBLEMS

Don't turn more than one dial at a time. Adjust the dial that appears too tight first, then TEST SEW. If the looper threads are imbalanced, do the same. Loosen the tight one first. If that doesn't solve the problem, return that dial to its original position and tighten the one that appears too loose. How do you know which is too tight? Read on . . .

HOW TO RECOGNIZE TENSION PROBLEMS

Diagnosis of tension problems is easy if you know what to look for. Remember the following:

1. The needle tension dial controls the **seamline**.

2. The upper looper tension dial controls the **top** side of the overcast.

3. The lower looper tension dial controls the **bottom** side of the overcast.

If your seam is pulling apart like this . . .   . . . tighten the needle tension.

If your seam puckers like this . . .   . . . loosen the needle tension.

If your stitch looks like this, loosen the upper looper and/or tighten the lower looper.   **If your stitch looks like this,** tighten the upper looper and/or loosen the lower looper.

HEAVY DECORATIVE THREADS BREAK TENSION RULES

To get a **balanced** stitch, each tension dial will be set at a different place when using a thick thread in one looper and a thin thread in the other. You will need to ignore the recommended settings in your manual.

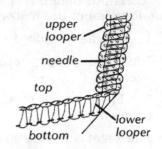

upper looper

needle

top

lower looper

bottom

The reason is that heavier threads create more **resistance** in the tension dials. A fatter thread simply **takes up more room**.

Decrease tension for thicker threads.

Increase tension for thinner threads.

If you loosen the tension on heavy thread completely and it is still too tight, try removing the thread from one or more thread guides. If that doesn't work, completely remove the thread from the tension dial as shown. **Experiment**!

If your machine has a "squeezie" guide at the top, remove the thread from it first.

OUR BEST TENSION TIP OF ALL!!

After teaching several four-day workshops, we discovered the obvious!! The WIDTH of the loops is controlled by tension. **Looper** width can be changed by loosening or tightening tension.

In this drawing of a balanced stitch, the loops, "hug" the edge of the fabric.

Here, we've loosened the looper tensions. The loops widen and hang over the edge of the fabric.

If you actually **change stitch width**, you will move the needle or knife blades. In addition, you will need to change the tensions as follows:

The **wider** the stitch, the **more** looper thread you'll need. Loosen both looper tensions and let more thread flow through.

The **narrower** the stitch, the **less** thread you'll need. Tighten the tension dials to let less thread flow through.

If you **widen** the stitch without loosening the tension, you may get the "pokies" on a woven fabric. The loops are too tight (narrow) against the edge. Loosen the looper tensions.

If you **narrow** the stitch width without tightening the tension, you may get "sloppy" loops or they may hang over the edge too far. Tighten the looper tensions.

When tension is **unbalanced**, a wide loop may even wrap over the edge. Often it is "pulled" over the edge by a narrow loop. Look at the following examples. Which loops need to be narrower? Which ones need to be wider? Always loosen the one that's too tight first!

Loosen (widen) the lower looper tension. You may then need to tighten the upper looper tension.

Loosen the upper looper tension. You may then need to tighten the lower looper tension.

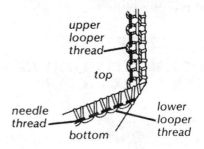

CREATE A REVERSIBLE EDGE

There are times when your heavy decorative thread will **only** work in the upper looper. To make the edge look the same on both sides, loosen the upper looper tension until it "wraps" the edge and tighten the lower looper tension until the lower looper thread disappears. With a 2-thread stitch, tighten the needle and loosen the looper. This is also called a wrapped edge.

STITCH LENGTH AFFECTS TENSION

If you maintain the same stitch width, but change the length, you will need to change the looper tensions as follows:

The **longer** the stitch, the more looper thread you'll need. **Loosen** the looper tensions so more thread flows through.

The **shorter** the stitch length, the less looper thread you'll need. **Tighten** the looper tensions so less thread flows through.

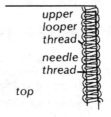

NOW THE BAD NEWS — HICCUPS!!!

Sue came up with the term "hiccups" for the narrowing of a stitch. This is caused by serging too fast, the thread getting caught in a thread guide, or the thread getting caught on the spool and not reeling off freely.

BUT THERE IS GOOD NEWS — HOW TO FIX HICCUPS!

1. Rip out stitching to just above the hiccup. Pick the needle thread with a seam ripper. You need enough needle thread to tie a knot. Begin new stitching without a chained tail (page 37).

2. Lower needle into seam line a few stitches above where you stopped ripping as shown.

3. When stitching is completed, go back to hiccup area and pull all threads to wrong side. Dab knots with a seam sealant like Fray Check®, Fray-No-More®, Fray Stop®, Fray Block®, and No-Fray®. Trim or bury threads in seam.

WHAT HAPPENS IF YOU RUN OUT OF THREAD?

If you are serging along and run out of thread, oh my! However, you can fix the stitching using the same steps for fixing hiccups. You may need to unravel some stitches to have enough to tie, but you won't need to rip out the entire seam.

Failsafe Fundamentals

CHAPTER 5

FAILSAFE FUNDAMENTALS

In this chapter we'll show you tips that can make a BIG difference in your serging (and sanity!)

REMOVING THREAD FROM THE STITCH FINGER
Frequently you will need to remove the chained tail threads from the stitch finger in order to pull on, release, or separate the threads. Use this technique for:

• Separating threads to check threading (page 26).
• Start neatly when sewing in a circle (page 40).

It's easy! Just pull slack in the needle thread between the needle and the tension guide as shown. Pull slightly for turning corners and a lot for separating threads. Many machines release the tension when the presser foot is up.

RIPPING IS EASY

• On a 2-thread overedge, pull on needle and looper threads equally and at the same time. They will pull out easily. Pull from the end, not the beginning of the stitching.

• On a 2-thread chain, pull on the looper thread and it will pull right out.

• On 3- and 3/4-thread stitches, slip a small seam ripper under the loops on one side, cutting them. The needle and looper threads on the other side will easily pull out. Or, simply pull on the needle thread and the loops will fall off.

needle thread

NOTE: Gail never rips. She just reserges, trimming of the edge... great for home dec when exact size isn't crucial.

KNOTTING NEXT TO THE FABRIC

Pati was a 10-year old 4-H member when she learned this neat trick for knotting next to the fabric. Our workshop students were awed by this simple method.

1. Tie the knot loosely. Slip a straight pin into its center.	2. Wiggle knot over pin until it gets close to fabric edge.	3. With pin at fabric edge, slip knot to point. Pull tightly.

SECURE THE END OF A SEAM BY HAND

The loose loops at the beginning or end of a seam can ravel out. You can't backstitch on a serger! Use one of the following methods to secure a seam: (First, smooth out the tail so it's not bulky.)

- **Tie a knot and put a dab of seam sealant** such as Fray Check® or Fray-No-More® on it. After it dries, cut off the excess chain. (Use rubbing alcohol to remove unwanted seam sealant).

NOTE: To make the seam sealant more "controllable", use a pin or your finger to dab it onto the knot. Sue puts hers into an empty nail polish bottle and uses the brush to apply it.

- **Bury the chain.**

1. Thread it through a large blunt pointed tapestry needle or a loop turner.	2. Pull the chained tail under the looper threads and cut off any excess.

SECURE THE END OF A SEAM BY MACHINE

It's easy and if you follow our instructions carefully, you won't get a loop of chained tail threads on the edge of the fabric as shown at the right.

• At the beginning of a seam

1. Stitch one stitch into fabric edge. Remove chain form stitch finger (pg. 37).

2. **Then** lift presser foot and bring chain to front. Run fingers along chain and pull to make it narrow.

3. Place chain on seam allowance and serge over it.

• At the end of a seam

1. Serge one stitch off the edge of the fabric. Gently slip the chain off stitch finger (pulling a slight amount of slack above needle will make this easier — see page 37). Raise presser foot. Flip fabric over and to the front of the presser foot.

2. Lower the presser foot and stitch 1"-2" over last few stitches. Be careful not to cut into the stitches already sewn. Chain off and trim the chain.

stitch finger

NOTE: Tighter looper tension and stretchy thread discourages raveling, i.e. a rolled hem stitched with woolly nylon thread requires no more than seam sealant.

STITCHING IN A CIRCLE

There are two ways to stitch in a circle. However, to entirely avoid serging exposed edges in a circle, use our sewing order, page 46.

- **Stitch over beginning stitches** 1/2"-1", then off the edge. Tie a knot near the fabric. Put seam sealant on the knot and cut off excess chain. This method can look messy unless you are using a thread that covers well, therefore, we generally reserve it for hem edge finishing.

- **Stitches meet without overlapping.** This gives neater results but takes practice!

1. Pull out unchained threads (see page 37), important if you want a tiny invisible knot.

2. Always begin serging in the **middle** of a long edge, NOT on a curve. **Always** skim the edges with your knives for even width serging. Stop serging when the knives reach the beginning stitches.

3. Disengage the knife and continue serging two stitches over the beginning stitches. Remember to replace the knife when finished.

4. Again, pull out about 3"-4" of unchained tail thread.

5. Tie knots in each tail. Dab knots with seam sealant, then cut off excess thread or weave tails into your serging.

foot

knife

NOTE: Use this technique if you have a seam allowance to trim. Cut away a 2" section of the seam allowance where you plan to begin and end your stitching. Then proceed as above, beginning in the middle of the cutaway.

begin serging here

TURNING INSIDE CORNERS

Inside corners are easier to finish than outside corners. Use the following technique.

1. Serge until the knife touches the corner. Stop with needle in fabric.

2. Straighten the corner, Lift presserfoot if necessary. You will have a "V" fold of fabric. Don't worry, the pleat will disappear after serging.

3. Finish serging the straightened edge.

4. Now the inside corner is finished!! It will appear a bit rounded.

NOTE: If your inside corner has a seam allowance that needs to be trimmed away, simply mark the cutting line within 1" of both sides of the corner using a washable marker. Clip to corner. Serge, as above, trimming off seam allowance.

cutting line

TURNING OUTSIDE CORNERS

Pati's mother-in-law learned to sew on a serger by making flannel receiving blankets. She got lots of practice turning corners! Try the following technique:

1. Serge up to the corner and off the edge ONE stitch.

1 stitch over the edge

2. Raise the needle out of the fabric. Raise the presser foot.

3. Pull a small amount of slack in the needle thread — a little finger's worth! This will help you remove the fabric from the stitch finger. Be careful. Too much slack will leave a loop on the corner. Experiment until you determine the right amount of slack required. If you accidentally pull too much, pull the thread back just above the tension dial.

stitch finger

4. Pivot the fabric. Lower the needle into the fabric BEFORE lowering the presser foot, or the needle won't end up where you want it! The needle should be in from the edge the same distance as the width of the seam allowance. Place it between the top edge and the seamline of the first stitching.

needle position

5. Continue sewing next edge.

NOTE: If there is a seam allowance, trim it away for 2" before serging to corner. Remember, your knife is in front of the needle, so you can't turn a corner without first removing the seam allowance!

cutting line

2"

CHAPTER 6
STABILIZING DECORATIVE SERGING

Serging is more durable and the stitch width more consistent when the edge or seam is stabilized. Without stabilizing, some exposed seams and edges, particularly on knits, can stretch out and ripple when serged, worn, or laundered. Gail noticed this on several of her daughter's single-layer tee-shirts; the serged necklines soon stretched or popped out. Our Serger Workshop students have also realized better results with stabilizing—more uniform stitches and less stretching.

Stabilizing isn't always necessary. If in doubt, test on scraps of your project fabric cut on the same grain.

STABILIZING DECORATIVE (EXPOSED) SEAMS

Before deciding whether a seam or edge needs stabilizing, consider the serging stitch. Most stable is the 4/2-thread stitch (chainstitch plus overedge), and the stretchiest are the 3/4- and 3-thread overlock. Generally, the wider the stitch, the more stable the seam.

> **NOTE:** A close satin stitch can cause stretching of a seam or edge, due to thread density.

To stabilize shoulder, neckline, front **seams** or seams in any problem area, try one of the following:

- Sew seam with a row of conventional straight stitching first, then serge seam allowances together. Or, add the straight row after serging.

- Serge using a 4/2-thread overedge/ chainstitch. (We have even seen **exposed** 4/2-thread seams on ready-to-wear denim!)

- Serge over braid, ribbon, yarn, buttonhole twist or pearl cotton.

- Flatlock over 1/8" braid or ribbon.

> **NOTE:** For additional stability, press serged seams to one side and edgestitch to garment to secure.

STABILIZING DECORATIVE (EXPOSED) EDGES

There are several ways to stabilize stretch-prone edges.

- **Facings** — Cut facings from self- or contrast fabric. Wrong sides together, serge to garment. After serging, leave the facing full width or trim to 1/2"-1". Interface facing with a lightweight fusible for extra body.

facing

- **Narrow self-fabric strips** — Serge 3/4"-1" strips of self-fabric to garment edges wrong sides together. Trim excess to serging. Use lengthwise grain for stability and bias when give is desired.

self-fabric strip

- **Fusible knit** or Perfect Fuse Sheer— 3/4"- 1" wide strips of a smooth fusible are great for adding **both** body **and** stability to an edge or to back an entire piece.

interfacing

- **Yarn, pearl cotton, buttonhole twist, elastic cord**—Serge over any of these. Tails can be drawn up, easing to fit. Secure tails with a knot and weave under loops on wrong side (see page 38). This technique

yarn

stabilizes, but doesn't add body. We prefer it when the silhouette demands softness like an angora sweater, or the fabric is stable like boiled wool. A special foot such as a tape sewing or cording foot makes this easier. Otherwise, practice feeding the cord through the hole of your regular foot, laying it just to the left of the knife. This is easier than placing it under the foot.

- **Ribbons** — Use ribbons only on straight or slightly curved edges. Place ribbon on wrong side of fabric and serge with ribbon on top. Avoid cutting the ribbon. Serge **over** narrow 1/8"-1/4" ribbon and **through** wider ones.

narrow   **wide**

Fast Flat Construction

CHAPTER 7
FAST FLAT CONSTRUCTION

Flat construction is perfect for single layer and reversible clothes. It eliminates serging in a circle. Start with casual tops, then serge ahead to jackets and coats!

SLEEVELESS ROUND NECK PULLOVER TOPS AND DRESSES

Use single layer (or double for reversible looks) of interlock, double-knit, single-knit, or lightweight woven fabric and the following sewing order.

Be sure to stabilize exposed edges if necessary. Serge fabric right or wrong side together as follows:

1. Serge one shoulder seam.

2. Serge to finish the neckline.

3. Serge the other shoulder seam. Then finish armhole edges.

4. Serge one underarm seam and then serge finish hem edge.

5. Serge the other underarm seam. Tie and bury any chain tail threads (see page 38). If desired, topstitch exposed **seams** flat.

"V"-NECKLINE PULLOVER TOPS

Add a center front seam to make continuous decorative serging easy on "V"-neck tops. Serge fabric right or wrong sides together as follows:

1. Serge both shoulder seams.

2. Serge finish the neckline.

3. Serge the center front seam right or wrong sides together, whichever you prefer. If you serge neckline and front in direction of arrows, serging can be continuous.

4. Serge armhole seams. Then stitch one underarm seam and serge finish the hem edge.

5. Now serge the other underarm seam. Tie and bury any chain tail threads (see page 38). If desired, topstitch exposed seams flat.

SINGLE LAYER JACKETS AND COATS

Who would have ever thought a jacket or coat could be as simple to sew as a blouse? Look for stable meltons, double-knit, double-faced or boiled wool, sweaterknit, or even upholstery fabric. Two medium-weight fabrics in contrasting colors can be used wrong sides together to simulate the look of double-faced fabrics. Use a balanced stitch and the same thread in both loopers or wrap the edge (see page 34). This will make the edge reversible.

GAIL'S FOUR-STEP JACKET OR COAT

Gail made this jacket from a very heavy wool melton which is inherently ravel-resistant, making the single layer garment very durable and easy to sew.

1. Decoratively serge finish the outer edges of the upper collar. Serge the shoulders and one underarm seam right sides together.

2. Starting at the lower edge of the open side seam, decoratively serge hem, front edge, collar to neckline, other front and rest of hem.

3. Sew the open side seam.

4. Decoratively serge finish the sleeve hem. Seam and set in sleeves.

VOILA! . . . a finished jacket!

MARTA'S LAPPED VARIATION

Palmer/Pletsch's resident sewing speed demon, Marta Alto, has devised another single layer sewing order for coats and jackets.

1. Decoratively serge finish all edges of collar.

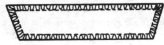

2. Serge shoulders and one underarm seam wrong sides together.

3. Starting at open side seam, decoratively serge finish jacket edges as shown. Serge other side seam wrong sides together.

4. Lap collar and neckline edges, aligning the serged needle lines. Topstitch collar to neckline with a conventional machine.

straight stitching collar

COORDINATE OTHER DESIGN DETAILS

We generally reserve dramatic **contrasting** decorative stitching for lapels, collars, and hemlines. However, when the color matches or is a subtle contrast, other design details can also be decoratively serged, like the edges of:

- Belts
- Patch pockets
- Sleeves
- Back vents
- Yokes

NOTE: Coordinate buttons too! See page 94 for the "wrapped" button.

Fun With Flatlocking

CHAPTER 8

FUN WITH FLATLOCKING

Flatlocking is serging two layers of fabric together, then pulling them apart until the seam lies flat. Since writing our first book **Sewing With Sergers,** we have experimented with flatlocking even more and have been amazed by the possibilities!

We'll show you how to flatlock with either a 2- or 3-thread stitch. A 2-thread flatlock will lie flatter, but a 3-thread stitch is possible.

Woven fabrics can be flatlocked, but they won't be as durable as knits when you use a narrow stitch width unless stabilized (see page 53). For your first flatlocking project, try sweatshirting or polar fleece. These fabrics are easy to sew, inexpensive, and durable.

FLATLOCKING IS REVERSIBLE

Depending on whether the fabric is serged right or wrong sides together, there will be **loops or a ladder** (trellis) on the right side.

For **loops** on the right side, flatlock fabric **wrong** sides together. Then pull until the seam lies flat.

For a **ladder** on the right side, flatlock fabric **right** sides together. Then pull until the seam lies flat.

2-THREAD FLATLOCKING

If your machine can sew a 2-thread stitch as shown at the right, you can sew a 2-thread flatlock. Check your manual. Opened flat it will look like the drawings on the bottom of page 51.

We recommend a balanced tension for a 2-thread flatlock. The needle and the looper threads should meet at the edge of the fabric. If using a heavier decorative thread in the looper, the tension may need to be loosened. Also, if you are flatlocking thick fabrics, both tensions may need to be loosened. Sew a test sample. If the flatlocking doesn't lie flat, loosen the needle and looper thread tensions until both hang over the edge slightly.

3-THREAD FLATLOCKING

The following steps allow you to flatlock with a 3-thread stitch:

1. Loosen the needle tension usually all the way and tighten the lower looper tension.

2. Do this until the needle thread forms a "V" on the under side and the lower looper forms nearly a straight line on the edge.

NOTE: If you have tightened the lower looper tension all the way and still can't get the lower looper thread tight enough, use Woolly Nylon in the lower looper. Loosen the tension, then gradually tighten while serging slowly so you won't bend the lower looper.

Flatlocking will always appear flattest when the loops and the ladder are the same width. If one side buckles under the stitches, loosen that tension dial. Do not **overpress** to try to flatten the stitches!

CREATIVE THREAD IDEAS FOR FLATLOCKING

Frame the stitch — When the loops are on the right side, use a contrasting color thread in the needle of a 2-thread stitch or the needle and lower looper of a 3-thread stitch. Your loops will be "framed".

Float the stitch — When the loops are on the right side, use clear filament nylon or matching lightweight thread in the needle of a 2-thread stitch or the needle and lower looper of a 3-thread stitch. The loops will seem to be "floating" on top of the fabric.

Define the ladder — When the ladder or trellis is on the right side, it will always be soft because only lighter weight threads can be used in the needle. Try topstitching thread, Designer 6, or Decor 6 for a more defined ladder.

FLATLOCKING FABRICS THAT RAVEL

It is easiest and neatest to flatlock on knits because they don't ravel. Even stable wovens may eventually ravel after many wearings and washings. Using a wider stitch width will help prevent raveling. You can use one of the following methods to stabilize them:

Method I

1. Sew flatlock seam.

2. **Gently** pull seam flat and press.

3. Fuse 1" strips of Easy Knit fusible tricot interfacing to the wrong side, centered over the stitches.

4. If more strength is needed, top-stitch from the right side through all layers on both edges of your serging. This will prevent ravelling during repeated washings.

METHOD II

1. Fold seam allowances to wrong side and press. Serge edges of seam allowances.

2. Serge the fabric right or wrong sides together, depending on whether you want the loops or the ladder on the right side of the garment.

3. Pull the layers until the seam is flat. Lightly press.

4. As an added decorative touch and for more durability, topstitch the seam allowances flat on both sides of the serging.

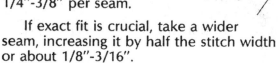

HOW FLATLOCKING AFFECTS FIT

If you flatlock with the needle in the seamline, then pull the seam flat, the garment width will be increased by the width of the seam allowance or about 1/4"-3/8" per seam.

seam line   seam line

If exact fit is crucial, take a wider seam, increasing it by half the stitch width or about 1/8"-3/16".

stitching line   seam line

FLATLOCK ON THE FOLD FOR A TOPSTITCHED LOOK

Flatlock anywhere on a garment including on a fold. You can even flatlock across flatlocking! Use decorative thread for more stitch definition. This is a great way to dress up sweatshirts or tops **and** to practice your flatlocking.

Fold the fabric and flatlock, being careful not to cut the fold with the serger knives. Place the fold halfway between the needle and knife. We use the knives as a stitching guide. They force us to sew straight.

Loops out	Ladder out

FLATLOCK OVER RIBBON

Flatlock on the fold over ribbon. 1/16"-1/8" width works well because the ribbon should be slightly narrower than the stitch.

ribbon

This is a great look on blouses and also a pretty embellishment for children's clothes.

Apply rows to a bodice or just above a ruffle.

FLATLOCK GATHERING

Narrow, center-gathered ruffles are a nice accent above a flounce on a full skirt or curtains. The ruffle edges can be beautifully hemmed before gathering using a narrow rolled serged hem.

1. Fold fabric in half, right sides together. Serge over cording, being careful not to cut the fold.

2. Pull up the cord and open ruffle. Stitch to fabric on both sides of cord or zigzag down the middle with a conventional machine.

FLATLOCK SHIRRING

Fold the fabric and flatlock over elastic cord.

Pull up on the elastic. Flatlock shirr your fabric first.

Then cut out your pattern. This is great for children's clothes.

ROLLED EDGE FLATLOCK

Change to a narrow rolled edge stitch. Adjust machine for 2- or 3-thread flatlocking. Flatlock on the fold. The result will look like soutache topstitched onto your fabric. "Frame" the stitch by using contrasting color thread as described on page 53.

FLATLOCK FRINGE

This is a wonderful finish for scarves, shawls, skirt hems, placemats, and napkins. It looks great when serged with decorative threads. The Coats & Clark educational staff showed us square wool challis print shawls they had flatlocked with black pearl cotton . . . gorgeous and much more finished looking than plain fringing.

Choosing the right fabric is a must. How does the fabric look fringed? Is it loosely woven enough to be easily fringed? If not, choose a more suitable fabric. TEST fringe a scrap first.

To flatlock fringe, do the following:

1. Draw a thread to find the straight of grain on the fabric where your fringe will begin, about 1"-3" from edge.

$1"-3"$

2. Fold your fabric on the drawn thread line.

3. Adjust your serger for flatlocking. Test length and width. Flatlock along the fold of the fabric being careful not to cut the fold (see page 55). As you serge, let the stitches hang halfway over the edge to allow the fabric to pull flat without a tuck forming underneath the stitching.

4. Flatten the stitches by pulling on them. Then, fringe to the stitching by gently pulling out all threads lying parallel to the flatlocking.

TURNING CORNERS WHEN FLATLOCKING ON THE FOLD

Whether flatlocking or flatlock fringing, use the following steps for turning corners:

1. Draw threads on all edges to be fringed as described on page 57. Fold the fabric under on drawn thread line and flatlock on fold, beginning where drawn thread lines intersect. Remember, do **not** cut the fold or your fringe will fall off!

2. When you reach the next drawn thread, raise the presser foot. When turning corners you usually need to loosen the needle thread at this point, but in flatlocking, the needle thread is already loose. Raise the needle and gently slip the stitches off the stitch finger.

3. Carefully open the first stitching and pull flat. Fold next edge under on drawn thread line. Lower needle in top of first stitching line as shown. **Then**, lower presser foot and flatlock to next drawn thread. Repeat these steps until all edges are finished.

4. On the last edge, stop serging immediately after overlapping the other stitches. Raise the presser foot and the needle. Pull enough slack in the needle to remove the stitches from the stitch finger and pull fabric from machine. Allow enough thread tail length for tying and burying under the stitches.

5. Pull edges flat and fringe to stitching as on page 57.

FLATLOCK DESIGN IDEAS

As a design variation, serge more rows of flatlock topstitching (see page 55) parallel to the flatlocked fringe. Also, vary the look and save time by flatlocking and fringing only one or two sides of a project. For instance, on an oblong scarf, flatlock fringe the short ends first, then finish the longer sides with rolled edges. A skirt hem requires only one row of flatlocked fringing — plus no corners.

FLATLOCK FAGOTING

True fagoting is accomplished by pulling horizontal threads out of a fabric and tying the remaining vertical threads together in hour-glass bunches as shown.

You can achieve a similar look with the serger. For a delicate handcrafted look, use this technique to join layers of lightweight cotton or handkerchief linen. Use clear nylon thread in upper looper of a 3-thread stitch or in the lower looper of a 2-thread stitch.

1. Serge to finish seam allowances and press to wrong side. Right sides together, flatlock with loops hanging halfway over the edge of fabric.

2. When you pull the seam flat, there will be an even width space between the layers.

3. Weave a shiny 1/8" satin ribbon in and out of the fagoting as a variation.

stitch finger

The Perfect Rolled Edge

CHAPTER 9

DECORATIVE ROLLED EDGES MADE EASY

One of our favorite features on a serger is the rolled edge. Garments like blouses are now easy to sew and professional looking. Save money on children's clothes and use self-fabric ruffles instead of lace. Gail, the home decorating expert, now uses the rolled edge to neatly and quickly finish curtain tiebacks, tablecloths and napkins, and ruffled pillows. It is also very durable because the fabric actually rolls under.

Our first book describes rolled edge basics. Now we want to elaborate on the how-tos, the decorative uses of the rolled edge stitch, and the problems you may encounter when venturing on to more challenging fabrics and threads.

SETTING UP YOUR MACHINE

Regular   Narrow

stitch finger

stitch finger

seam allowance

knife

You will need a narrow stitch finger to sew a rolled edge. On some machines this adjustment is built-in; on others you need to change throat plates. You may also need to change to a special presser foot. Check your manual.

The edge of the fabric actually rolls under because the distance between the knives and the stitch finger is greater than the width of the stitch by at least 1/8".

Set your stitch width to 2.5–3.5mm. We recommend **gradually** shortening the stitch length until you get the look desired. Most people prefer a satin stitch, but beginning on a very short length may cause uneven feeding of the fabric and a lumpy edge. TEST on a sample first!

Fabric is always placed on your machine right side up except when serging a fabric that rolls to the right side like crosswise grain tricot. Why fight it? Place it right side down.

NARROW EDGE VERSUS A NARROW ROLLED EDGE

In machine manuals, you see the terms narrow edge and narrow rolled edge. There is a difference. In both cases the fabric rolls because of the distance between the knife and the narrow stitch finger. However, the narrow edge does roll a bit less. The difference is caused by tension adjustments.

On a **narrow edge** the stitch is balanced. The upper and lower looper threads of a 3-thread stitch and the needle and looper threads of a 2-thread stitch meet at the edge.

For a **narrow rolled edge**, the stitch is unbalanced. The upper looper thread of a 3-thread stitch and looper thread of a 2-thread stitch encases the edge.

TENSION ADJUSTMENTS FOR A 3-THREAD ROLLED EDGE

Lower looper — The greatest tension adjustment is on the lower looper. By tightening it nearly all the way, the lower looper thread will become a straight line on the wrong side of the fabric and nearly disappear. It also pulls the upper looper thread to the underside.

Tighten lower looper a lot.

NOTE: If you cannot get the lower looper tight enough to completely wrap the edge, try Woolly Nylon in the lower looper. It is like making the tension 2-3 numbers tighter. If you have Woolly Nylon in the upper looper, you will need to loosen the tension. Woolly Nylon in the needles and both loopers gives great coverage and strength.

Upper looper — It may need a little tightening or loosening, but depends on the type of thread and fabric used as well as stitch length. Since decorative threads are generally used **only** in the upper looper, TEST on a sample first.

No change but test.

Needle — The needle thread tends to loosen under the strain, so you may need to tighten the tension. If it becomes **too** tight, however, the edge may pucker. TEST on a sample first. Puckering most often occurs on the lengthwise grain of fabric.

Tighten needle a little.

The following drawings show you how a rolled edge is formed:

As you tighten the lower looper tension, the upper looper is brought to the wrong side.	As the lower looper becomes tighter, it can create stress on the needle thread. Tighten it.	Perfect! The upper looper has been pulled all the way to the under side and the needle thread is hidden.

lower looper thread

bottom

needle thread

bottom

bottom

lower looper thread

TENSION ADJUSTMENTS FOR A 2-THREAD ROLLED EDGE

If your serger sews a 2-thread stitch and can make a rolled edge, try it for a lighter edge finish. Bridal veils are often finished this way. Adjust your machine for a rolled edge per your instruction manual.

Tighten the needle tension until the looper thread rolls from the top of the fabric to the underside and encases the edge. If the fabric is heavy, you may need to tighten the looper also to make the fabric roll.

Narrow edge—
Balanced 2-thread tension

looper thread

needle thread

bottom

Narrow rolled edge—
unbalanced 2-thread tension

needle thread

looper thread

bottom

DECORATIVE ROLLED EDGES

variegated threads

Make a rolled edge more decorative by using a contrasting or special thread. Rayon, silk, and metallics add shine. Woolly Nylon adds texture and gives good coverage. Variegated threads are beautiful because they "color block." Generally, finer threads (extra fine, serger or regular thread) are better. However, you can try topstitching thread or pearl cotton #8 for more definition. Heavy rayon thread like Decor 6 or Designer 6 are beautiful on an edge. TEST them using a longer stitch length. Generally, it is necessary to loosen the upper looper three numbers if Woolly Nylon is used.

ROLLED EDGE STITCH VARIATIONS

Picot, Shell, or Scalloped Edge

This look, commonly seen in lingerie, is formed by lengthening the stitch to 4 or 5. If the fabric puckers, loosen the needle tension. The fabric should be held taut both in front and behind the presser foot to prevent puckering.

Mini Blanket Stitch Look

Loosen the needle and tighten both loopers nearly all the way. Both looper threads will be on the edge of the fabric and the needle thread will show on both sides. Lengthen the stitch to 5mm. The result will look like a narrow blanket stitch. Try this with lightweight decorative threads in the needle and loopers.

Lettuce Leaf Edging

This ruffled or "lettuce" effect can be interesting on belts, aerobic wear and skirts. Create a lettuce effect with any narrow or rolled edge set on a short satin stitch length. The degree of ruffling is based on the amount you stretch the edge while you sew. Also, the following will affect stretch:

- Use stretchier fabrics such as single knits and jerseys.
- Lightweight fabrics will lettuce more than heavy weight.
- Crosswise grain in knits and bias in wovens will stretch more.
- The shorter the stitch length, and the stretchier the thread (such as Woolly Nylon), the more lettucing.
- Increase presser foot pressure to increase stretching.

CREATIVE USES FOR THE ROLLED EDGE STITCH

Rolled Edge Scallops

This technique is great for fabrics or lace.

1. Trim away seam allowances on scallops.
2. Disengage knife. If you can't, don't try this technique. Serge edge of scallops with rolled edge stitch. When you reach the inside point between scallops, straighten the fabric as you would for an inside corner (see page 41). Do not stretch.

Attaching Laces and Trims

Use the rolled hem stitch to attach laces and trims for a corded edge appearance. Place lace and fabric wrong sides together and serge together with the rolled hem stitch. Use a 2mm stitch length.

wrong side

Decorative Belt Loops or Lattice Work

Create decorative strips of fabric for belt loops or lattice work. They can also be woven together for pillows, handbags, yokes and other accents.

"lattice"   **belt loops**

1. Cut long strips of fabric 1" wide. Later the strips can be cut into the lengths needed. Interface to prevent stretch if necessary. Fuse the strips wrong sides together with fusible web for extra body and for easier handling.

2. Serge along one edge with a rolled edge stitch. Turn the strip around, making sure the same side is on top. Align the first stitching with the left side of your presser foot for even width strips. Serge the other side.

3. Cut the strip into lengths desired.

Make Your Own Trim

When you can't find trim to match your fabric, make your own. Use lace, eyelets, cotton blends—the sky's the limit!

1. Cut strips of fabric the width desired plus a seam allowance. If gathering the trim cut it three times the finished length.

2. Serge one edge with a rolled edge stitch. Attach to garment flat or after gathering.

Create Your Own Piping

By making your own piping with the rolled edge stitch, you will be able to match almost any color of fabric. You can create an unusual lightweight look not available in purchased piping.

1. Use 1 1/4" Seams Great®, Seams Saver®, or bias cut strips of chiffon.

2. Place one to three strands of filler cord such as pearl cotton in the center of the strip.

3. Serge over the filler threads with a satin rolled edge stitch, trimming close to cording.

VOILA! Piping! Insert while sewing a seam or facing an edge. Using a zipper foot, stitch close to piping. See our **Sensational Silk** book for complete piping instructions.

NOTE: You may prefer to fold strip **over** filler threads and serge. Be careful not to cut the fold. This adds additional body to the piping.

CREATIVE USES OF THE CHAIN TAIL THREAD

The rolled edge chain itself looks very nice, especially when using a heavier thread like topstitching thread. Every time you use the rolled edge stitch, serge an extra yard for belt carriers, button loops, or spaghetti straps.

Belt Loops

Pull on the chain to smooth out the loops. See our book **Sewing With Sergers** for tips on attaching chain belt loops.

Filler Cord

If you want your rolled hem stitch to be fuller and stiffer, use a matching length of chain as a filler cord. Smooth out excess loops in the chain by pulling it taut. Place the chain on top of the fabric and serge over it with a rolled edge stitch.

ROLLED EDGE SEAMS CAN BE DECORATIVE

Seams Out

Try seaming lightweight fabrics wrong sides together using a rolled edge stitch. Decorative matching or contrasting threads are lovely.

Serge with the two layers of fabric wrong sides together. To prevent raveling, a short stitch length (satin stitch) is best.

Seams in Sheers and Laces

Rolled edge seams look gorgeous showing through sheers and laces. These are considered decorative because they show. Gail likes to use Woolly Nylon for softness and better thread coverage. Marta prefers regular thread or rayon with a 2mm stitch length.

SOLUTIONS TO ROLLED EDGE PROBLEMS

Students in our workshops seem to have some problems over and over. Because they are common, we'd like to address them here.

Stitches Do Not Cover the Edge

This is most common when the thread and fabric are different colors. Shorten the stitch length; try two strands of regular thread in the upper looper; or use Woolly Nylon as it fluffs and spreads to fill in the spaces between the stitches. Two blending threads of Woolly Nylon create an interesting look.

Stitches Pull Away From the Edge of the Fabric

If the fabric is loosely woven, the rolled edge may pull off the fabric. This happens most often on the crosswise grain of the fabric. Lengthening the stitch will help as fewer needle holes will be punched into the fabric. Also, use the smallest needle available for your serger.

Another option is to move the knife farther away from the stitch finger so that more fabric is being rolled into the edge. This can be done on most machines; however, consult your owner's manual.

Our last resort is to serge over tricot to stabilize as shown on page 69. Trim tricot to seamline when finished.

The Rolled Edge "Pokeys"

"Pokeys" are little fibers sticking out the edge like whiskers. This most often happens with heavier or stiffer woven fabrics that resist rolling. Try moving the knives to the right so more fabric rolls under. Check your owner's manual to see if this is possible.

"pokeys"

To prevent pokeys, serge over water-soluble stabilizer (on top side). For lined projects, such as napkins, fuse the edges together first, then serge finish the edge.

It is almost impossible to control "pokeys" on metallic wovens. Place a strip of sheer tricot such as Seam Saver or Seams Great or a wash-away stabilizer such as Solvy on **top** of the fabric and serge through all layers. Trim the excess tricot close to stitching with embroidery scissors.

trim away excess tricot

When all other attempts fail, try folding under the raw edge about 3/8" to the wrong side. Align the fold just to the left of the knives. Being careful not to cut the fold, serge along the edge.

Using sharp embroidery scissors, trim away the excess fabric to the stitching.

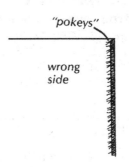

"pokeys"

wrong side

Reverse "Pokeys"

When you see pokeys on the **inside** of the rolled edge, it means too much was rolled into it for the type of fabric you are working with. If possible, move the knives to the left, so more fabric is trimmed.

Rolled Edge Puckers

Loosen the needle tension. Try a smaller needle. Hold fabric taut as you sew. Also, if the stitch length is too short, the stitches will stack on top of each other and sometimes cause puckers.

If you do not let the machine trim at least a small amount off the edge, you will have spots with less fabric in the roll and it can cause unevenness and puckers. Therefore, **always** let the knives trim off a small amount.

Fabric Won't Roll

If the fabric is stiff or heavy, it may not roll. It will scrunch instead, resulting in the "pokeys." You can tighten the upper looper, forcing a roll. If that doesn't work, loosen your upper looper and you will eliminate the pokeys, but produce a wider edge finish.

Rolled Edge is Stiff and Heavy

If you want a lighter rolled edge, use a lighter weight thread such as rayon, silk, machine embroidery thread, or extra fine thread. You can also lengthen the stitch to reduce the density of the thread. Use a stitch length of 4 on scarves for a soft edge.

Rolled Edge is Not Consistent in Density and Width

A rolled edge sometimes looks different in the lengthwise and crosswise grains. There is not much you can do about this (although we have come up with a solution for napkin edges on page 116). Preshrinking fabric to remove sizing sometimes promotes more even rolled edge stitching.

The serger always rolls the edge of the fabric down. If your fabric wants to roll up, it will fight the machine and produce an uneven edge. Don't fight it. Place the fabric on the machine so it will roll down.

Dog-eared Corners

You can turn corners with a rolled edge, but generally we just serge off, then begin on the other edge and cross over our first stitching. To secure threads, use a seam sealant on the corners. After it dries, trim off the tails. The sealant is not water-soluble, so the project will be washable.

To avoid dog-eared corners like this, use Gail's trick.

As she approaches the corner, she angles in the last three or four stitches, about 1/8".

Then, on the next edge, she begins stitching in a little (about 1/8"), then angles back out. The finished appearance is a perfect right-angled corner.

Heirloom Sewing

CHAPTER 10

HEIRLOOM SEWING

The art of French hand sewing has been revived and it is all the rage among needle artists. When worked on by hand, as it was in the Victorian era, the intricate scheme of lace inserts, pintucks, and entredeaux required hours and hours of painstaking sewing.

In this chapter, we'll show you how quickly and beautifully serging can simulate French hand sewing. We call it "heirloom serging." You'll love the results for feminine blouses, frilly childrenswear (christening gowns are gorgeous), and for accents such as yokes, pockets, or hankies.

CHOOSING A PATTERN

Styles with minimal darting and seaming are best. Also, generous design ease will afford larger garment sections for heirloom serging. Decoratively serge the fabric first, then lay out the pattern and cut out the garment. Remember, fit the pattern before cutting it out.

HEIRLOOM FABRICS

Heirloom sewing was traditionally worked on delicate Swiss batiste or organdy. Lightweight wovens such as batiste, organdy, and handkerchief linen are widely available today. Recommended fabric color choices for heirloom projects are white, ecru, or pastel colors. Trim and fabrics should be color-on-color such as white on white or pale pink on pail pink. However, on white you can occasionally add a hint of pastel ribbon or stitching.

FINE THREADS WORK BEST

Finer threads are best for delicate heirloom serging. Try serger or extra-fine machine embroidery thread. A hint of shine from rayon and silk thread can be very pretty. Serge a TEST sample first to check suitability of thread with fabric, trims, and stitches used. Avoid any thread that breaks easily during testing!

TRIMS, LACES, AND RIBBONS

Many laces, trims, and ribbons will serge beautifully. When choosing a lace, it should be soft, but have body; washable, if used in washable garments; the same weight, or heavier than the fabric; and wider than the serger presser foot to avoid bunching. We also like narrow 1/16"-1/8" ribbons under a flatlocked stitch for an accent. The following are some of our favorite laces and trims:

Entredeaux (on-trah-doe) — a trim with 1/16"-1/8" wide holes similar to hemstitching. For serger sewing, choose one with fabric borders. Use it between strips of fabric or other laces or trims.

Beading — can be either a lace or embroidered trim. It has openings through which ribbons can be inserted. Try a narrow pastel ribbon for a hint of color.

Lace Insertion — has a straight edge on each side. Packaged lace seam binding is a common example of lace insertion.

Lace Edging — has one straight edge and one scalloped edge. Use the scallop to finish a hem edge.

Untrimmed Eyelet — makes great lace insertion. The untrimmed edges will be straight after serging. Adjust the finished width of the trim as desired.

Fabric Puffing — made from a strip of garment fabric, gathered on **both** long edges and used as an insertion. For a slightly puffed insert, start with a fabric strip twice the finished length. For full puffing, use a strip three times as long.

ESTIMATING LACE AND TRIM YARDAGE

To estimate the yardage of each lace and trim you plan to use, determine the length of each row and multiply by the number of rows. Plus, buy extra for practice and boo boos. The pattern envelope may be of some help if it gives back length and hem width measurements.

STITCHES USED IN HEIRLOOM SERGING

- **2- or 3-thread rolled edge stitch with a stitch length of 2mm—** can be used for:

  inserting laces and trims   **pintucking** (use the width of the presser foot as a guide)

- **Flatlocking** — can be used for:

  joining lace to lace or lace to fabric (loops or ladder can be on right side)   **flatlocking on the fold** (generally done with the ladder on the right side)

- **Chainstitch** — if your serger will sew a chain, use it to decorate ribbon. With decorative thread in the looper, place the ribbon right side down and sew through the center of the ribbon. Then serge the ribbon to the garment.

- **Regular serged seam** — can be used for sewing tucks (use a wide width satin stitch) or for joining decorative work.

- **Decorative stitches on a conventional machine —**

  To fill in spaces between rows of lace or pintucks, use ribbons, topstitched in place, or rows of embroidery stitches such as flowers, sewn on a conventional machine.

CREATING HEIRLOOM YARDAGE

It is easier to create heirloom yardage first, then cut out your garment. Estimate fabric yardage the same way we suggested estimating yardage of laces and trims. Add an extra 8" of length for blips and boos boos.

If you are creating yardage just for a collar or a yoke, your strips of fabric and trims should be at least 4" longer than the widest part of the garment piece. This allows for shifting of trims as you serge.

The following tips will save your sanity when creating heirloom yardage:

- All stitching should be done on the lengthwise grain or puckering may occur.

- "Test see" a design by laying strips of the trim, lace, and ribbons over the fabric. Re-arrange until you are satisfied. Note the center, spacing, and order of rows.

- Lightly mark trim placement lines with a water soluble marker.

- As you build the design, start in the center and add trim to the left, then the right. Do not build all of one side, then try to repeat it on the other side. Both sides would be guaranteed to look different!

- Always sew with lace or trim on top so upper looper thread is in same place on both sides. You will sew from bottom to top on one side and top to bottom on the other.

- If you have a stitching problem and need to rip, remove the entire row of stitching. If the stitching is on the fold like pintucking or flatlocking, be careful not to cut the fabric or you will end up with a hole and the area will be too weak to hold up after restitching.

SEWING ORDER

The following is a sample of a sewing procedure used to create heirloom yardage:

1. Draw center line and insertion lines on fabric with water soluble marker.

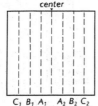

2. Cut on line A_1 and insert trim.

3. Cut on line A_2 and insert trim.

4. Cut on line B_1. Insert trim. Then cut on line B_2. Continue until all trim is inserted.

PATTERN LAYOUT

After you have created your heirloom yardage, lay pattern tissue over the design. Shift the pattern over the stitching to determine which placement works best. Cut each garment piece single layer. Don't forget to flip the pattern for a right and left side unless the design is asymmetrical.

CHAPTER 11

RIBBING

Ribbing, the functional finishing for tee's and sweat-shirts, is now seen in the most fashionable places — on wool doubleknit dresses, woven silk blouses, and designer leather jackets. This stretchy knit finishing knows no gender. It's versatile for men's, women's and childrenswear.

Ribbing is synonomous with serging. Study ready-to-wear ribbing applications. Most are serged. Like the ribbing, serging stretches. Plus, narrow serged seam allowances are lightweight and inconspicuous, perfect for body-fitting ribbed fashions.

With the following tips, anyone can be a ribbing expert. You'll find many creative uses for fast-to-serge ribbing. Have fun!

CHOOSE THE RIGHT RIBBING!

When a ribbing application looks homemade, the culprit is generally the ribbing, not the seamstress. Read through this section before shopping and at least you won't **buy** a problem!

• **Avoid sloppy ribbing by TESTING resiliency.** Simply stretch the ribbing firmly. Does it return to its original size? If not, look for another. Words of wisdom from our ribbing expert, Naomi Baker, "Ribbing that stretches out and doesn't stretch back will **always** be ugly no matter how well you sew!"

• **Investigate fiber content.** Care requirements for the ribbing and garment should be the same. Ribbing choices are many— 100% cotton, cotton/Lycra®, cotton/polyester, nylon, acrylic, acrylic/polyester, acrylic/wool, and 100% wool. The ones that are most resilient are cotton/Lycra r, cotton (incredible stretch recovery, but hard to find and less ribbed looking), 100% nylon (can be "plastic" feeling), acrylic/wool (the more wool, the more resilient) and 100% wool (gorgeous, versatile, and spendy).

- **Combine similar weight fabrics and ribbings.** If the ribbing is heavier, it will overpower the fabric. If the ribbing is too lightweight, it won't have the body and resiliency to control the edge. Our favorite ribbing/fabric combinations are wool ribbing on wool doubleknit or silk charmeuse. We also like cotton/polyester ribbing on cotton/polyster interlock knit. Experiment!

- **Know how ribbings are sold.** Most commonly available are 24"-60" wide tubular **ribbings sold by the yard.** 1"-4" wide **ribbed bands** with one finished edge are also available and often coordinated to yardage. Gail's favorite finish for crew neckline tee-shirts is a ribbing band folded wrong sides together and applied double layer for extra body. Rib knit collars are real timesavers, and not for polo shirts only.

Often striped or finished with interesting edgings like picots, rib knit collars are great for perking up a solid color fabric. Buy three collars — one for the neckline and two for the cuffs.

- **Be creative if you can't find MATCHING ribbing.** Consider contrasting colors. Black is elegant on most brights. White is a nice accent on a print. Gail salvages ribbing by trimming it off worn or outdated clothes (some are thrift shop finds). She also knits her own ribbing, especially nice for heavy woolens, leathers or leather-likes.

DO NOT PRESHRINK RIBBING.

Preshrinking ribbing makes it soft and much harder to handle. Only lengthwise shrinkage if any will occur, not significantly affecting the stretch or fit.

RIBBING RATIOS

Ribbing should hug the body and keep the edge of the garment from stretching. Generally all ribbing is stretched at least a little when applied, even to a straight edge. The more curved the edge, the more you will need to stretch the ribbing to make it lie flat and hug the body. Knowing how much to stretch ribbing becomes intuitive for ribbing enthusiasts. Unfortunately for beginners, there are no absolute rules, because there are too many variables.

Ribbing stretched the right amount. Hugs the body.

Ribbing not stretched enough. Stands away from body.

For neckline ribbing that hugs the body, follow these general guidelines:

Round necklines — Cut ribbing 2/3 the size of the neckline and pin in place distributing ease evenly.

Oval necklines — Cut ribbing 3/4 the size of the neckline. Place most of the stretch over the shoulder area. For 5"-7" across center front and back, stretch ribbing only 1/2"-1".

stretch 1/2"-1"

For "V" necklines — Cut ribbing 3/4 the size of the neckline and stretch only slightly down the front.

For turtlenecks — Cut the ribbing the same size as the neckline or slightly less if very tight.

MAKE SURE THE RIBBING WILL FIT

Common sense is a good guide for fitting ribbing. Simply pin the ribbing into a circle and try it on. Does it fit easily over your head, wrist, or waist?

SUE'S TIPS FOR SERGING RIBBING

Sue teaches ribbing application in our serger workshops. Her many helpful hints include:

- **Use either a 3- or 3/4- thread stitch** because they have the most give. Use a medium stitch length and medium to wide width.

- **Lift the presser foot** and put the layers of ribbing and fabric under it. Lower the presser foot and begin sewing.

- **Always serge with the ribbing on top,** with the exception of "V" necklines. See page 83.

- **Follow a flat construction sewing order** to avoid serging in a circle. See pages 82 and 83.

- **When applying ribbing over other serged seams, reinforce those seams** for 1" on a conventional machine. Since a narrow seam allowance is used to apply ribbing, seams can "pop" where they meet ribbing.

- **Trim all seam allowances on ribbing and garment to 1/4".** This makes it easier to apply ribbing evenly.

- **If you goof, rip out stitches** or in many cases you can serge again, trimming off the first seam. It will make your ribbing narrower, however. You may also serge over first stitching to even up an uneven seam.

- **Press minimally.** Touch the iron to seam allowances only. Pressing can stretch some ribbing. Press over a ham, steaming the ribbing to shape of neckline. Let ribbing cool before moving.

- **Do not use seam sealant** to secure the ends of neckline ribbing seams. When it dries it will be scratchy! Gail discovered this when her daughter, Bett, complained. Knot close to the fabric instead (see page 38).

CIRCULAR RIBBING APPLICATION

This is the most common ribbing application, popular in tee shirts and also used on cuffs and waistlines. Our students prefer this tidy technique. The ribbing is seamed in a circle first, then serged on.

1. Cut the ribbing to size.

2. Right sides together, seam the ribbing with a conventional straight stitch. Finger press open.

3. Fold ribbing wrong sides together. To distribute ease evenly, quarter both ribbing and neckline.

4. Match the pins and serge, stretching ribbing to fit garment edge. **Remove** pins as you serge.

5. To end the seam, overlap stitches for about 1"-2", then taper off the edge.

FLAT CONSTRUCTION IS FASTEST!

1. Serge one shoulder seam.

2. Serge ribbing to neckline edge.

3. Serge other shoulder seam.

4. Serge ribbing to sleeve edges.

5. Serge sleeves to armholes.

6. Serge one underarm seam.

7. Serge ribbing to hem edge.

8. Serge other underarm seam.

For "V" Necklines

1. Serge one shoulder seam.

2. Serge ribbing to neckline with fabric on top to ensure catching the "V". Use inside corner technique on page 41.

3. Miter the "V" by folding it in half along center front. Machine baste on a conventional machine from serged needle line to ribbing edges. From the right side, make sure the ribbing seams and edges match. Then final stitch with a straight stitch.

4. Clip the miter fold and press back. Hand tack the raw edges flat to the serged seams.

5. Finish garment using crew neckline sewing order.

CREATIVE RIBBING IDEAS

- Lettuce the top edge of double-layer ribbing. Use a narrow rolled edge and Woolly Nylon thread. Stretch as you sew. Lettuce leaf ribbed socks to match!

- For the Esprit look, mix and match ribbing colors on top.

- Pants too short? Serge ribbing to the hem edge. Instant fashion.

- For the "hot hip" look band, cut ribbings super wide, at least 7" when folded in half.

- Apply right side of ribbing to the wrong side of garment neckline. The ribbing will fold over and hide serged seam.

CHAPTER 12
CREATIVE SWEATSHIRTS AND FLEECE

Sweatshirts are easy, fast-to-finish projects. What other garment could be serged decoratively in so many different ways? Sweatshirt fabrics are easy to handle and popularly priced! They hold their shape but are flexible enough to "forgive"less-than-perfect serging and fitting.

Don't have time to sew a sweatshirt? Combine decorative threads and stitches to jazz up plain ready-made sweatshirts available in both set-in and raglan sleeves and in a wide range of colors.

The Patterns

All the pattern companies now offer sweatshirt styles for women, men, and kids. Sweatshirt patterns are usually designed with few seams. Unseamed areas on the front and back give you a large area for decorative serging. Even the most basic pullover style can be transformed into a designer sweatshirt.

The Fabric and Ribbing

Sweatshirt fleece can be cotton, cotton/polyester, cotton/acrylic or 100% polyester (such as in popular "polar" fleece).

A wide variety of ribbing is finally available to the homesewer. See pages 78 and 79 for a detailed explanation of types, fibers and sewing techniques and why we **don't** preshrink ribbing.

Thread Possibilities

Because most of us wash, rather than dry-clean sweatshirts, decorative threads, yarns and ribbons used should withstand repeated washing and drying. Among the most durable are topstitching thread, crochet cotton, and Woolly Nylon.

Helpful Notions

There are several notions you will find helpful when creatively serging sweatshirts, including a water-soluble marking pen, ruler, and dressmaker's curve, seam sealant like Fray Check® or Fray-No-More® a seam ripper, and loop turner.

The Stitches

Several decorative stitches are appropriate for sewing creative sweatshirts. Our three favorite stitches for sweatshirts are:

Flatlock Stitch (pg. 51)	Framed Flatlocked Stitch (pg. 53)	Serged and Lapped Seam

NOTE: To make a decorative flat-felled seam, serge fabric wrong sides together with a balanced wide, medium-length stitch. Press seam to one side with decorative thread on top and topstitch seam flat through all layers on a conventional machine.

knife

DECORATIVE SERGING SEWING ORDER FOR RAGLAN SLEEVE SWEATSHIRT

1. Serge all but one back sleeve seam.

2. Add decorative serging. Try one of these ideas:

back   open

front

right side

flatlock on the fold

additional rows flatlocking

flatlocked seam

3. Then serge ribbing to neckline and sleeves.

4. Serge the back sleeve seam through neck rib.

5. Serge one underarm seam.

6. Serge the ribbing to the hem.

7. Serge other underarm seam.

DECORATIVE SERGING SEWING ORDER FOR SET-IN SLEEVE SWEATSHIRT

1. Decoratively serge pieces. Sew one shoulder seam. Apply neck ribbing.

2. Serge other shoulder seam. Set in sleeves. Apply sleeve ribbing.

3. Serge one underarm seam. Apply lower ribbing.

4. Serge other underarm seam.

The "Ski Sweater" Sweatshirt

By using your favorite raglan sleeve sweatshirt pattern, you can make a plain sweatshirt into a "ski sweater." A basic ready-made raglan sleeve sweatshirt is also simple to decorate. Consider different colors of thread on the same shirt.

Flatlocked rows.

Flatlocked rows alternating with decorative stitching sewn on a conventional machine.

Flatlocked seams in a color blocked design.

Ribbings attached with decorative flat-felled seams. Apply ribbing to wrong side of neckline. Topstitch seam flat with a double needle.

MORE CREATIVE IDEAS

Lettuce Edge Ruffling

1. Try on shirt and mark lettuce line first with pins. Then mark line with water-soluble marker.

2. Fold sweatshirt, wrong sides together, on marked line.

3. Stretch folded fabric and serge with a rolled hem stitch. Be careful not to cut the fold.

Fastest Color Splicing Ever

1. Use a striped fabric and flatlock along stripes.

2. **Then** cut out sweatshirt and sew together.

Random Flatlocking

Flatlock stitch at random on fabric before construction.

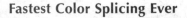

Mock Flatlocked Piecing

Use the same random technique for small areas such as yokes. Flatlock squares. Cut on bias. Mark first with a water-soluble marker.

Sensational Serged Sweaters

CHAPTER 13

SENSATIONAL SERGED SWEATERS

Undoubtedly you've admired the gorgeous, spendy sweaters now so popular in ready-to-wear, from casual cardigans to one-of-a-kind hand knit originals. Serging beautifully finishes cut edges, so even hand knits can be "cut and sewn" rather than assembled by hand.

For those without the time or talent to knit, sweaterknit yardage is now more accessible and affordable than ever before. Take an evening to serge a sweater that would surpass any expensive readymade in styling, fit, finishing and durability.

HAND KNIT OR CROCHET YOUR OWN SWEATER KNIT YARDAGE

For our cut-and-serge method, stick with fine to medium gauge yarns, generally no bulkier that four stitches per inch. Fibers like cotton, wool, linen, acrylic, and blends thereof ravel less than do slippery silks and rayons. After creating the yardage, cut out your sweater using a pattern.

After knitting, blocking is essential to stabilize and prevent raveling. Blocking is steam pressing the yardage to square it into shape. Follow the yarn label instructions. Generally no additional stabilizing of edges is required before cutting, but if you are unsure, zigzag within the seam allowances before cutting. Or, you can actually stabilize the entire piece with textured weft interfacing like PerfectFuse Light **before** cutting out.

WHICH SWEATER KNITS CAN BE SUCCESSFULLY SERGED?

Whether you buy, make or recycle sweater knits, look for these desirable characteristics:

Fine to medium gauge — The finer the gauge, generally the more stable and ravel resistant. A guide for machine and hand knits would be a gauge no larger than four stitches per inch. Bulkier sweater knits can be serged successfully, but testing is required.

Four or more stitches per inch are easiest to serge.

wrong side

Raschels, other loosely constructed knits or openwork knit laces can present some challenges when serging. They may require slower stitching to prevent catching the fibers on the foot, stitch finger, and/or upper looper.

Yarns that aren't too slippery or nubby—Large slubs or loops catch on the foot, needle or upper looper. Slippery yarns or ribbons can slip as your serge.

Smooth stitch patterns — Pronounced stitch patterns like cables can be bulky, but usually can be flattened enough with the foot for smooth serging.

CUTTING SWEATER KNITS

Allow 1/2"-1" wide seam allowances. Serging edges can cause what is termed "waves over the ocean" or undesirable stretching. The excess can be trimmed off or finished.

If the ribbing is knitted in, place the sweater hemline at the ribbing edge. Stretch the ribbing to form a straight line. Secure with pins or weights. When the ribbed edge springs back after cutting, it will hug body contours.

SWEATER KNIT SEAMS

Test, test, test! Never serge along the seam edges. Trim away at least 1/4" to minimize stretching. To decrease bulk at intersecting seams, alternate the direction of the serged seam allowances. The heavier the knit, the wider and longer the stitch should be to prevent waviness. Also, lighten the presser foot pressure for heavier bulkier knits. If the seam is still wavy, ease the fabric with your fingers in front of the presser foot as you sew or serge.

Woolly or stretch nylon thread is a good choice for sweater knits. This soft, yarn-like thread buries itself in the sweater texture, effectively securing the stitches.

Use one of the following to stabilize shoulder seams:

Serge over tricot scripts — Sue uses Seams Great® or Seams Saver® on openwork or loosely constructed sweater knits.

lining stabilizer

Use 1" wide strips of the selvage edge of lining fabrics — Gail's favorite method for shoulder seams. It is soft, non-bulky, and available.

Serge over ribbon or clear elastic.

Use a stable stitch

Most stable ◄———————————————————► Stretchier

Sew first with a conventional straight stitch. Then serge seam edges together. This is our favorite for hand and machine knits.	A true 4-thread stitch has little stretch. Use it for shoulders or any seam that requires stabilizing, or where stretch is unnecessary.	A 3/4-thread stitch is nearly as stretchy as a 3-thread and adds a bit more strength to the seam.	A 3-thread stitch has the most give — perfect for sweater knit seams that require stretch, i.e., a turtle neck ribbing seam that will be stretched over the head.

MORE SWEATER TIPS

- Face a sweater knit with a woven fabric. Choose styles with lapels and roll-up cuffs so the lining **will** show! Allow an extra 3/8" on all seams for fitting ease. Wrong sides together, decoratively serge the sweater knit and lining together, using a balanced, decorative stitch.

- Accent sweater knits with lace trim, yardage and appliques. Serged seams "show through" the lace always looking even and trimmed.

CHAPTER 14

QUICK PATTERNLESS ACCESSORIES

Need an accessory to wear tonight or give tomorrow? Take your pick!! Serging makes them incredibly fast.

FLATLOCKED AND FRINGED ACCESSORIES

Our serger workshop students **love** our scarves and shawls with flatlocked and fringed finishing. See pages 57 and 59 for step-by-step directions.

Experiment with decorative threads, yarns, or ribbons. For heavier fabrics like wools and boucles, consider yarns, pearl cotton, or easy-to-use buttonhole twist/topstitching thread. When flatlocking silks, Gail likes rayon thread or Woolly Nylon.

LARGE SCARF OR SHAWL

Flatlock and fringe all sides with a fringe depth of 1-2".

Suggested fabrics — printed scarf "squares" in rayon or wool challis, silk or silk-like faille, or charmeuse, or lightweight boucles.

40"-60" square yardage required:
40" x 40" size —
1⅛ yard of
45" + fabric.
60" x 60" size
1⅔ yard of
60" width.

MUFFLER

Flatlock and fringe short ends (depth, 1"-3") before finishing long sides with narrow rolled or decorative serging.

Suggested fabrics — light to medium weight wools, wool blends or acrylics (good for sensitive skin!).

9"

1/4 yard of 45"-60" width fabric.

45"-60"

TIES AND SASHES

Flatlock and fringe short ends before finishing the sides with narrow rolled serging. Braid three ties together for an unusual look.

yardage required:
1/4 yard of 60" fabric
1/2 yard of 45" or wider fabric (piece in center)

REVERSIBLES

Line flatlocked and fringed accessories with lighter weight fabric in a contrasting color. Fringe the single layers first. Then place the wrong sides together. For square scarves, straight stitch the two layers together about 1/8" in from the fringing. For oblong mufflers, ties and sashes, fringe the short ends of both layers, then serge the longer edges together using a decorative narrow rolled edge.

yardage requirement
same as above for
both fabric and
lining

NOTE: See our book, **Sewing With Sergers**, for other scarf sizes and styles.

CHAINSTITCHED AND SERGED BELT

Janet Klaer, Sew News columnist, showed us a nifty belt that can be sewn entirely on a serger. Use contrasting color lining to create a reversible belt. (You need a serger that will sew a chainstitch.)

Suggested fabrics

Light-to medium weight fabrics like linen or linen-likes and silks or silk-likes.

1. Cut two belt pieces, about 3" wide by your waistline measurement plus 16". For waist sizes to 29", 45" width fabric affords enough length for a belt. For thicker waists, piece with a serged seam to achieve the desired length.

waist
measurement
plus 16"

3"

2. Sandwich a layer of polyester fleece between the wrong sides of the fabrics.

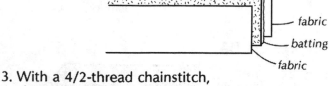

fabric

batting

fabric

3. With a 4/2-thread chainstitch, channel quilt the layers together, alternating stitching direction to prevent grain distortion. To keep rows even, use the presser foot width as the distance between rows. Try using pearl cotton or other decorative thread in the looper and stitch the belt right side down.

4. Finish the belt edges fast with 2- or 3-thread narrow rolled or balanced serging. If decorative thread was used for chainstitching, use the same thread for the edging and taper the ends.

ONE-SIZE-FITS-ALL BELT

1. Cut a strip of synthetic suede like Ultrasuede® Brand Fabric, or dressmaker weight leather. You'll need a piece one quarter yard wide by at least 44" long. Add body by making the belt double layer. Except for true leathers, you can fuse the layers together with fusible web. One layer can be a contrasting color.

44" or longer

about 4½"

2. Finish the edges with decorative serging.

square

tapered

rounded

3. Taper or round off the ends as desired.

4. You're almost finished. Thread belt ends through a buckle, one at a time. Adjust to fit.

completed belt (worn with ends in or out)

SOFT TOTE IN SECONDS

Finish the edges of three 16" squares with narrow rolled edge serging. Durable, tightly constructed cotton or cotton blend wovens work best.

Straight stitch the scarves right sides together, using a 1/8" wide seam allowance along the serged needle line.

Assemble as shown. Tie the unseamed corners into a square knot.

seams

Great for toting knitting, kids' toys, beach attire or gym clothes!

Serging Specialty Fabrics

CHAPTER 15

SERGING SPECIALTY FABRICS

The serger can handle nearly every fabric, but some require special handling.

SHEERS AND LACES

Fabrics that are sheer and semi-sheer should be sewn with a narrow serged seam. Because the distance between the needle and knives is always the same it will look totally even in width from the right side. The rolled hem width is nearly invisible from the right side like a French seam. (See page 69.)

DOTTED SWISS AND EYELETS

Both of these fabrics have raised motifs which can cause irregular serging stitches. This is normal. When finishing with a rolled edge, avoid serging over the raised areas, stitching between the motifs when possible.

VELVETS

For velvets that are thick and ravelly, sew a conventional 5/8" seam and serge the seam allowances single layer to finish. Carefully press the seams open over a velvet pressing board or self fabric.

KNIT OR WOVEN METALLICS

Narrow seams in knitted metallic fabrics will hold up under stress better than in a woven. Test serge a seam in a scrap before beginning project. Serging edges with a matching metallic thread can be sensational. Some metallics may require a serged French seam (see page 104) to prevent the fabric edges from irritating the skin. For rolled edges on metallics, fuse very light fusible strips to the wrong side of the edges before serging to prevent ravelling.

QUILTED FABRICS

Two layers of quilted fabrics are sometimes too thick to easily feed into and be cut by serger knives. The knives only open about 1/4", so quilted fabrics thicker than 1/4" will bunch up in front of the cutters and jam.

5/8" seamline

To compress quilted fabrics before serging, use a conventional machine to zig-zag with a long, wide stitch within the seam allowance next to the seam line. Then serger needle in the seamline. This keeps the edges of all the layers perfectly together.

For additional strength in quilted garments that will get lots of wear and laundering sew a "mock flat felled" seam. Serge, then press the quilted seam allowance to one side and topstitch through all layers on a conventional machine.

TERRY CLOTH

Terry cloth is a loosely constructed fabric. A serged seam alone will not be strong enough to withstand stress and repeated launderings. The following special seam for terry cloth is flat, decorative, strong, and reversible:

5/8" seamline

1. Serge each single layer with a wide, short stitch, trimming away 1/4" of the seam allowance.

NOTE: Make sure the **upper** looper thread is on the right side of the overlap side and the wrong side of the underlap side so seams will be reversible.

trim
1/4"

2. Overlap edges.
   Topstitch one edge
   through all layers.

seamline

3. Turn over and topstitch
   other edge through all
   layers.

seamline

REAL AND FAKE FURS

Fur is too bulky to be sewn with a regular serged seam. Also, the knives would cut the pile. Furs are sewn by professional furriers with a special machine that butts the edges together and sews from one side to the other. We can use a flatlock stitch to simulate the furrier's technique on real and fake furs.

1. Trim away the seam allowances. Brush the fur away from the edges toward the right side and place the pieces right sides together. Flatlock.

2. Pull the two pieces to open flat. On the right side, carefully pull out any fur caught in the seam. When working with real fur, reinforce by hand stitching 1/2" twill tape over the seam on the wrong side.

twill tape

SEQUINNED FABRICS

The following tips should help when sewing sequinned fabrics:

1. Cut out garment pieces single layer with the pattern on the wrong side of the fabric.
2. Cut through the backing fabric and sequin threads only; avoid cutting sequins. I" seam allowances are recommended.
3. Carefully unstring sequins from the seam allowances and save.
4. Using a fabric glue like Sobo, secure sequin thread ends to the edge of the seam allowance.
5. Serge seam allowance edges over the sequin thread ends and dried glue. Do not cut away the glue spots.
6. Sew the garment seams on a conventional sewing machine using a zipper foot in order to stitch close to sequins.
7. Carefully press seams open. Test first. Some sequins may discolor or melt with heat.
8. Hand sew leftover sequins to bare spots over the seam line on the right side of the fabric.

CHAPTER 16
LINGERIE

Beautiful lingerie is a wonderful addition to any wardrobe and a most welcomed gift. Quickly serged, lingerie sewn at home duplicates the finest readymade underfashions.

THE FABRICS

Cut tricot fabrics with the greatest stretch (usually the crosswise grain) going around the body.

Cut the woven fabrics, like affordable polyester "silkies" or luxurious silks, on the bias. Bias cut woven fabrics allow some "give", but will not stretch as much as a knit. Allow for this when cutting out the garment by using I" seam allowances for fitting "insurance".

THE SEAMS

NOTE: Use a medium serger stitch length for all the seams. Hold the fabrics taut in front and behind the foot to prevent puckering.

A standard narrow serged seam is an excellent choice for lingerie. Three-thread, 3/4-thread, and 4/2-thread sergers all make a strong, neat lingerie seam.

For a seam without bulk, try a flatlock stitch (page 52). The seam will lie flat and be inconspicuous under the clingiest skirt or blouse. If using a woven fabric, press under seam allowances before flatlocking.

For a narrow fine seam, use the rolled edge stitch (see page 61), and a 2.5mm length. Because tricots and bias wovens don't ravel, the seam will be strong. Test first. If additional strength is needed, see page 69.

Try "seam locking" with a 2-thread stitch — This is used by some manufacturers.

1. Tighten the needle tension until the needle thread forms a straight line on both sides of the seam.

2. Loosen the looper until the looper thread encases the edge of the fabric. See page 13.

For a durable seam in woven fabrics, try a French seam. It is sewn twice and is very durable, even in loosely constructed fabrics. A French seam is a 3-step process on a conventional machine, but on a serger it is a 2-step process. The following serger instructions are for a 5/8" seam allowance:

1. Set the serger on a 3.5mm stitch width.

2. Place the fabric wrong sides together and serge a seam, allowing the knives to trim away 1/8" of the seam allowance.

3. Press the seam allowance to one side. Press again, encasing the serger seam inside the fabric.

4. On a conventional sewing machine, sew a straight stitch seam 1/4" from the fold (through both layers of fabric), encasing the serger stitch.

right side

1/8"

conventional machine stitch

wrong side

first stitching encased inside

APPLYING LACES AND TRIMS

Laces and trims can be applied using either a standard serger seam or a flatlock stitch. Stitch all seams with the lace on top so you can see how close the knives trim.

To apply laces and trims with standard serger seams:

1. Place fabric and lace right sides together allowing the fabric to extend approximately 1/8" beyond the edge of the lace. The lace may be taped to the fabric or attached with a temporary hold spray like Sulky 2000.

2. Serge the lace to the fabric, trimming away the extended 1/8" of fabric. Be careful not to cut the lace. By trimming the fabric as the lace is applied, you will not miss the fabric under the lace.

right side

1/8" of fabr trimmed a

3. Press the seam allowance toward the lace so the seam will always lie flat.

1/8" of fabric trimmed away

wrong side

To apply laces and trims with flatlocking:

1. Place fabric and lace wrong sides together, allowing the fabric to extend 1/8" beyond the edge of the lace.

2. Flatlock (see page 51) the lace to the fabric trimming away the 1/8" of fabric as you sew.

3. Open and pull the seam flat.

To apply ribbon and lace simultaneously with flatlocking:

ribbon

wrong side

I. Place fabric and lace wrong sides together, with the lace on top. Allow the fabric to extend 1/8" beyond the edge of the lace.

2. Place a narrow (1/16"-1/8") ribbon on top of the lace at the seam edge. Flatlock over the ribbon, encasing it as the lace is serged to the fabric.

right side

ribbon

3. Open and pull seam flat. The ribbon will be under the flatlocked stitching, on top of the lace.

NOTE: The ribbon will stabilize the finished edge, so do not use this accent if the area needs to stretch for wearing ease.

To insert lace with flatlocking:

Insert lace by flatlocking it to the fabric, then trimming away the fabric underneath. Insert the lace before seaming the garment together. This technique is best on a tricot knit.

1. Mark placement lines for lace with a water soluble marker.

2. Center the lace over the placement line on the right side of the fabric.

right side

mark line / placement and center lace over line

3. Fold the fabric wrong sides together, with the lace on top.

4. Flatlock the lace to the fold being careful not to cut the lace or fabric.

5. Repeat on the other edge of the lace.

6. Open and pull the seams flat.

7. Carefully trim away the fabric under the lace with embroidery scissors.

trim fabric from wrong side

APPLYING ELASTIC

Simply quarter the elastic, match to quarter marks on the garment, and stretch to fit as you sew. You may also consider quartering the elastic and the garment again into eighths, to make it even easier to control while serging.

NOTE: You will find it easier to handle the elastic when the garment is flat (before seaming in a circle). To do this, leave a side seam open, apply the elastic and then sew the other side seam. See sewing order on page 108.

1. Place the elastic under the foot, aligning the right edge just to the left of knife. Serge about three stitches into the elastic to secure, stopping with the needle down. Lift the presser foot.

2. Slip the fabric under the elastic wrong side up. Allow 1/8" of the fabric to extend beyond the edge of the elastic.

3. Stretch elastic between marks and serge the elastic to garment, trimming 1/8" of fabric away. Serge SLOWLY, STOPPING WITH THE NEEDLE DOWN WHEN THE ELASTIC NEEDS STRETCHING. Continue to serge until elastic is applied.

4. Lightly press the seam allowance towards the garment.

1/8" of fabric to be trimmed by serger as you sew

right side

Always test a sample of elastic and fabric to check the stitch width and length. A longer than average (3-4mm) stitch length adjustment will prevent the stitches from bunching together when the elastic relaxes.

TO APPLY LACE TRIM AND ELASTIC IN ONE STEP:

1. See step 1 on page 106.
2. Place the wrong side of the lace on the right side of the fabric. Slip lace and fabric under the elastic. Allow the fabric to extend 1/8" beyond the lace and elastic.
3. Flatlock the lace and elastic to the fabric, stretching the elastic as you sew.
4. Open and pull the seam flat.

LINGERIE STRAPS

Ribbons, lace, and fabric strips make lingerie straps a snap. If color matching ribbons to fabrics is a problem, use strips of the garment fabric to make a quick spaghetti strap (see **Sewing With Sergers**, page 80).

For a quickie strap:

1. Cut 1/4"-1/2" ribbon the finished strap length, plus 2".
2. Cut two pieces of single edge lace trim the same length.
3. Use a flatlock or rolled hem stitch to apply lace to both long edges of the ribbon.

FAST SEWING ORDER FOR CAMISOLE AND TAP PANTS

Create simple elegance on edges of a camisole and tap pants by finishing with a rolled hem (or picot stitch) and rayon, Woolly Nylon, or machine embroidery thread. Variegated shades are lovely.

For Camisole:

1. Serge one side seam.

2. Finish the hem edge and top of bodice with a rolled hem stitch.

3. Serge the other side seam.

4. Make and apply straps.

For Tap Pants:

1. Serge center front and center back crotch seams.

2. With a rolled hem stitch, serge openings, as shown.

3. Bring the side seam together and serge using the rolled edge stitch.

4. Apply elastic to waist edge before serging the other side seam.

5. Finish the remaining side seam

NOTE: Fast sewing orders for half slips and panties are given in our first book, **Sewing With Sergers.**

CHAPTER 17

CREATIVE ACTIVEWEAR AND SWIMWEAR

More and more homesewers are serging activewear and swimwear. The increased interest is no doubt due to the popularity of serging. Our workshop students marvel at serging leotards in an hour or less. After mastering the basics shown in **Sewing With Sergers**, move on to these creative serging ideas.

We like Woolly Nylon or similar brands (see page 19) best for serging aerobic and swimwear because it is very strong and holds the seams well. Plus, it is soft . . . great for body fitting fashions.

INSIDE OUT FASHION

Activewear and swim wear can be worn wrong side out! The serged elastic application looks like a cover stitch when worn on the outside. All the rage among the fitness set, these leotards can also be worn right side out for a more traditional look.

Use contrasting thread. Experiment with different stitch widths and lengths . . . generally a medium to wide balanced stitch works best. For more color density, serge again over the first stitching.

For armholes, necklines, and leg openings, serge the raw edges with the contrasting color thread, turn up and topstitch the elastic casing. Or, use the cover stitch like they do in ready-to-wear. Or, serge the elastic to the raw edge, then turn up and topstitch. See page 87 in **Sewing With Sergers** for more details.

serge twice
for thread density

Serge the side seams with the same contrasting color thread. They become quite narrow in stretchy aerobic wear and look more like a design line.

MORE DESIGN IDEAS

- **Line two-way stretch leotards and swimsuits** with the same fabric in a contrasting color. The additional layer doubles the wearing mileage, smoothes the figure, and makes the garment reversible. Sew the fabric and lining separately. Place the two layers wrong sides together and join when applying elastic to the edges.

- **Try a double needle** for topstitching the elastic casing. It is more durable and a great look — often seen in ready-to-wear!

- **Lettuce edge** belts, ruffles, and necklines (page 65).

- **Add ruffles** to a neckline or insert them into a seam. Finish with a rolled edge stitch (see page 61).

- **Color block** or splice tights. Teens love different legs! This look is wild and the price is right, because only one yard of fabric is usually required. Using strong Woolly Nylon thread, flatlock the seams together to minimize bulk or use a cover stitch.

NOTE: Another look popular with the aerobic set is stirrupless capri length tights that can also be color blocked. Simply trim the stirrups off and finish the bottom edge with a serged satin stitch.

- **Two-way stretch fabrics make gorgeous pareus.** Buy 1-1/4 yards more of your swimsuit fabric. Finish edges with narrow rolled satin serging. Tie on for an instant dress or skirt, as shown.

ACTIVEWEAR HEADBANDS

All exercisers — golfers, tennis players, and joggers love "sweat"bands. Fishermen and hunters are kept warm with wool headbands. Serge them by the dozen — fast! Use prefinished ribbing, ribbing yardage, or two-way stretch fabrics. Buy fabric or recycle ribbing about 12" long and 2-3" wide (the stretchier, the better). Vary the style with the type of ribbing used.

Two-way stretch fabric headbands

These headbands are in demand for aerobics enthusiasts. They are easy to make because they only require one seam and can double as pull-on belts (for small waists only!). Use cotton/spandex (Lycra®) blend knits for comfort and absorbency.

1. Cut two pieces of two-way stretch fabric as shown.

2. Loop the pieces of fabric together. (Don't worry about the raw edges — the knit doesn't ravel and automatically curls under like an instant hem!) Place ends of each loop wrong sides together. Stretch to fit your head and mark seamline.

3. Serge the four layers together.

21"

5"

greater
degree of stretch

cut two

Medium weight ribbed yardage headbands

1. Fold ribbing in half lengthwise, wrong sides together. Flatlock the seam (see page 51) and pull flat.

2. Stretch it around wearer's head until it is snug, but comfortable. Mark seamline and serge.

Variation: Add a twist before seaming, as shown.

Medium to heavy ribbed band headbands

NOTE: This type of ribbing has one finished edge.

1. Cut a single layer and finish the one raw edge with medium to wide balanced serging. Trim at least 1/4" off the raw edge while serging to prevent stretching.

finished edge

2. Stretch to fit head, mark seamline and serge.

CHAPTER 18

CREATIVE IDEAS FOR CHILDREN

When it comes to kids' clothes, sergers are indispensable. Finally, you'll sew fast enough to keep up with those fast growing bodies.

The childrenswear you serge instantly (well, almost!) will look better and last longer than any ready-mades. Both Pati (daughter, Melissa) and Gail (daughter, Bett) have noticed that their serged "custommades" stand up to repeated washings!

SERGER SHORTCUTS

Replace bindings — on jackets and vests with decorative serging. If the garment is reversible, use a stitch that looks the same, or is decorative, on the upper and lower looper.

Create your own trim — the cost savings are substantial. Finish one or both of the edges with a narrow rolled edge. If there is enough fabric, cut the fabric strips on the bias for softness and stitch uniformity. For ruffles, use differential feed set at 2 and attach the ruffle with a shirring foot.

Shirr with serging. Thank goodness Sue Green developed this technique — it's the only shirring Pati or Gail have time to finish. Shirr the fabric before cutting out the garment. (See page 56)

Make frilly blouses and dresses fast!
Pin tucks are perfect. Experiment with fine shiny threads like rayon and different stitch lengths.

1. Tuck the fabric before cutting out.

2. Press mark the tuck fold lines.

3. Plan serging direction so the top side of the stitch will always show on the right side.

4. Serge along the fold line with a narrow rolled edge or a narrow balanced stitch.

finished
draw   pintuck   serge on
lines   fold

QUICK-TO-SERGE KIDSWEAR IDEAS

Serge children's swimwear, leotards and tights. Chances are if you've sewn your own, there will be enough yardage left over for a wee one. (See page 110.)

Serge Halloween get-ups! Buy preprinted costumes that glow in the dark. No more facings or bindings. Anxious Halloween goblins love the super-fast process.

Serge reversibles. Simple silhouettes like tee-shirts and jumpers are perfect candidates. (See page 82.)

BABY'S BOUNTY

Serged diapers! Choose super absorbent 100% cotton terry (preferred in England where they're called "nappies"), special diaper flannel, or knits. Simply serge finish the edges. Use two to four layers, depending on the fabric weight.

Sizes: 11" x 13 1/2" for infants to nine months. 13 1/2" x 16 1/2" for toddlers.

As a starter set, most babies need at least three dozen or about 2 1/2 yards of 45" fabric for infants and 5 3/4 yards of 45" fabric for toddlers.

Serge blankets! Look for 100% cotton flannel or soft acrylic sweaterknits. An ample size is 45" x 45" or 1 1/4 yard of 45" width fabric. For newborn babies, 30" x 40" receiving blankets are nice. Make them double if using flannel. Finish the edges with baby yarn in the upper looper. Or use #8 pearl cotton in both upper and lower loopers.

Blanket variations!

Add a protective hood to one corner. When made in terry cloth, this is the perfect after-bath "robe".

14"

hood

14"

Flatlock satin blanket binding or ribbon to the edges. Pati's new daughter Melissa has adopted a satin-edged blanket as her favorite.

4"

Make our favorite no-tie bib.
You'll need one fringed guest towel about 11" x 18" and 2" wide cotton or cotton blend ribbing that is about 16" in length.

1. Fold the guest towel as shown. Trim out the neckline opening using a large cereal bowl as a guide.

2. Cut the ribbing 4"-5" shorter than the neckline edge measurement but large enough to fit over the child's head (See page 80).

3. Seam the ribbing and serge to the neckline, evenly distributing the ease (See page 80).

seam at
center back

neckline
opening

right side
towel

CHAPTER 19

HOME DECORATING AND CRAFTS

No time to sew? Satisfy your creative urges and make your home more beautiful with these super-fast-to-serge projects.

NAPKINS

Somehow **cloth** napkins transform any meal into a dining occasion. Plus, serging napkins is a productive way to perfect decorative stitching, particularly the rolled edge. Gail's **first** serger project was 75 napkins...every one was serged with a different tension!

There's not an easier to make nor more welcomed gift than cloth napkins. Dive into your fabric stash ... good chance there's a cotton or cotton blend perfect for napkins. Unlike 100% synthetic readymades (Pati's pet peeve) they'll really absorb!

Yardage Estimates

	Quantity	Fabric Widths	
		45"	60"
18" x 18" (dinner size)	Four-Six	1 yard	1 yard
	Eight-Ten	2 yards	1½ yards
15" x 15" (size of most readymades and the most economical to make from 45" width fabric)	Four-Six	7/8 yard	7/8 yard
	Eight-Ten	1⅜ yards	1⅜ yards

Serging Tips

- Chain off at corners.It's the fastest and easiest method. Serge finish lengthwise grain edges first, then the crosswise grain The lengthwise grain has less tendency to pull out at the corners where the edge finishing intersects. Dab Fray Check® or Fray-No-More® on corners. Allow to dry, then snip. We know a restaurant owner who has her 400 home-serged napkins laundered and pressed daily. After a year, she hasn't detected noticeable fraying at the corners. To avoid dog-eared corners, see page 71.

- Experiment with thread types. Woolly Nylon is our favorite choice because it spreads to cover a rolled edge beautifully and minimizes fraying at the corners. Other thread types we like for finishing include: cotton covered polyester; buttonhole twist or topstitching thread; rayon thread, especially variegated; metallics for holidays; or two strands of all-purpose or serger thread.

- Experiment with stitch types. Although a rolled edge (pages 68-71) remains the most popular and durable finish for cloth napkins, a balanced stitch is a refreshing look. Use buttonhole twist in both the upper and lower loopers.

Creative Ideas

- Line with coordinating or contrasting fabric. Serge edge finish as one layer. Lining is a clever way to tie together related, but not matching, prints and colors. Many of our workshop students like to work with self-fabric so that the wrong side of a print won't show.

Also, to strengthen edges, align crosswise and lengthwise edges. Rolled edges will be more uniform on all four sides.

NOTE: Gail often fuses the napkin and lining together, before serge-finishing, preventing "pokeys" and ensuring stitch uniformity.

- Make strip patchwork napkins. Serge the strips together, then straight stitch the longest strip to the napkin, right sides together, as shown. Fold the strip triangle down, enclosing the seams. Serge finish the napkin edges.

- Have fun folding cloth napkins — even kids love to do it!

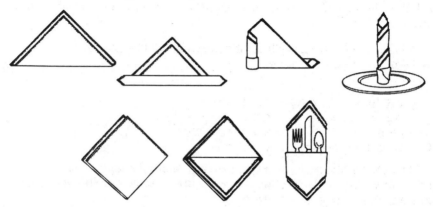

PLACEMATS

Placemats are handy for everyday use and a snap to serge! Make a set to match your napkins. Only one yard of 45" wide fabric will yield six 14" by 16" placemats. Use your favorite ready-made placemat as a pattern.

Yardage estimates — Yardages are given for single thickness only and for 14" by 16" size. Double the yardage for reversible or lined placemats.

Quantity	Fabric Widths	
	45"	54"
Four...................	1 yard	1 yard
Six.....................	1 yard	1 yard
Eight..................	2 yards	1½ yards

Fabric tips — Use double-sided quilted fabric for super-quick placemats. Just serge the edges and you're done! For firmer placemats, try these layering strategies:

Single-sided quilted fabric **plus** fusible web **plus** single-sided quilted fabric.

Single-sided quilted fabric **plus** fusible web **plus** fabric.

Fabric **plus** batting **plus** fabric with fusible web between the layers.

fusible web

All the above may be channel quilted with conventional straight stitching.

NOTE: For batting, we like bonded fiberfill like Stacy's Thermo Lam® or Pellon® Fleece.

Serging tips — Facilitate continuous serging by rounding off corners. Use a cup as a template. Trim with a rotary cutter. Or cut placemats in an oval shape.

If batting-filled placemats are too thick to feed into the knives smoothly, compress the layers first with a wide, long conventional zigzag, then serge edge finish.

Use the "belly button" rule — start serging in the center of the bottom edge of the placemat. Less-than-perfect lapping of the serging will be hidden under the dinner plate!

If you can't use a heavy thread in the lower looper, yet want the placemats to be reversible, wrap the edge. See page 34. Or, use pearl cotton in upper looper and topstitching thread like YLI's Jeans Stitch or #12 by Sulky in the lower looper.

Make flatlocked and fringed placemats (see page 58). Choose loosely woven linen looks and put your television watching troops to work fringing!

Thread types — Experiment with different threads. On heavier, multi-layer or quilted and stitched placemats, we like heavier threads such as pearl or crochet cotton or topstitching thread used in both loopers with a wide, balanced stitch. On thinner, single layer placemats, try Woolly Nylon, all-purpose, and rayon threads in a medium width balanced stitch. A rolled edge can also be used, giving a unique look to lightweight placemats.

PILLOWS

Make tie-ons for square pillows. The tie-ons should

tied on

tacked on

Finish ruffles with rolled edge. For extra body, make ruffles double layer using self-fabric or a contrasting color.

Make instant pillows! Serge edges of each piece separately, then straight stitch together 2" from edge for a flanged look. Leave a 4" opening for stuffing.

Flatlock fringe squares of fabric. Stitch together leaving a 4" opening for stuffing.

QUILTS AND CRAFTS

A version of vintage "crazy quilts" — flatlocked patchwork simulates hand worked feather embroidery stitches. Topstitching thread, fine yarn and pearl cotton are recommended. Block quilts are easiest and fastest.

1. Plot the patchwork color scheme.

2. Flatlock all parallel rows in one direction. (It may be necessary to compress layers first with a wide, long zig-zag stitch.)

3. Chain between blocks as shown. Then flatlock all rows in the opposite direction, trimming off the chains between rows.

4. Tuft through all layers and edge finish with decorative serging.

Use your quilted fabric for quilts, handbags, garments, doll accessories, and pillows. Let your imagination go!

Transform your serger into a stripping machine! — Remove the needles and thread. Mark the desired width from the knife on the front guard plate. Align the fabric edge with this mark as you feed fabric through serger to cut strips. This stripping method is a welcome relief for hands tired from cutting yards and yards of rag baskets, rag knitting, "rag point" and braided rugs.

CHAPTER 20

TROUBLE-SHOOTING

Problem	Solution
• **Skipped Stitches**	• Replace a bent, dull or damaged needle. • Use a needle the correct size for the fabric and thread. • Thread correctly, through all guides and eyes. Thread can easily come out of the open thread guides. The looper **or** needle tension may be too tight. Loosen one then the other to see which works. • Change needle size. • Insert needle correctly. The eye of the needle must face **exactly** toward the front of the machine. • Increase the presser foot pressure for heavier fabrics.
• **Puckered Fabric** (also, see Pg. 125)	• Hold fabric taut as you sew. • Loosen needle thread tension. • Adjust foot pressure. *Differential feed is on .7.* • Check for correct threading. • Shorten the stitch length.
• **Excessive Stretching** (also, see Pg. 125)	• Lighten the foot pressure. *Differential feed is on 1.5 or 2.0.* • Lengthen stitch • Stabilize edge. (See page 44) • Serge in from the edge, trimming off at least 1/4". • Be careful not to stretch fabric as you sew.
• **Irregular Stitches**	• Thread correctly.. • Change thread type.. • Replace with a new or different size needle. • Insert needle correctly. • Adjust tension. • Change to correct size needle for thread or fabric. • Check for proper cutting action of knives. **NOTE:** If the texture of the fabric is uneven, irregular stitches will occur. It is difficult to compensate for this.
• **Fabric Doesn't Feed Well**	• Presser foot is up. • Lengthen the stitch. • Increase or decrease foot pressure depending on fabric weight. • Clean lint out of feed dogs. • Check knife blades for excessive wear.
• **Thread is Breaking**	• Check for thread caught on spool notch, thread stand or guides on machine. • Rethread machine in proper threading order. • Balance the tension settings. • Insert needle correctly. • Loosen tension on the breaking thread. • Change the needle. • Use a high-quality thread.

Problem	Solution
• **Needle Breaks**	• Change to a new needle. • Insert the needle correctly. • Change to a larger size needle. • Check for thread caught or trapped in a thread guide. • AVOID EXCESSIVE PULLING OF THE FABRIC WHILE SERGING.
• **Machine Jams**	• Pull thread tails to the back as you begin to serge. • Make sure fabric trimmings fall away from, not into, the serger. • Lengthen stitch, especially if using heavy threads. • Close protective front cover while serging. • Serge fewer layers of fabric or compress thick layers. • Check for proper cutting position of knives.
• **Seam Pulls Open to Expose Stitches**	• Tighten the needle tension, or • Loosen the lower looper tension. • Check to see if thread is engaged in the tension dials.
• **Excessive Machine Noise**	• Clean and oil machine. • Insert new needle. • Check alignment of knife blades. • Consult your dealer if problem persists. **NOTE:** Check to see if the surface that the machine is sitting on is making the noise.
• **Trimmed Edge is Ragged**	• Reset knife blades correctly. • Change to a new blade. • Allow machine to trim at least 1/8" off the fabric edge.

SELECTING THE PROPER WIDTH, LENGTH AND NEEDLE SIZE

Weight/Stitch	Fabric Type	Width	Length	Needle Size
Light	Voile	2.5mm	2.0mm	12 (80)
	Gingham	3.5mm	2.5mm	12
	Georgette	1.5mm*	2.5mm	12
	Sheer	1.5mm*	2.5mm	12
	Lace	1.5mm*	2.0mm	12
	Silk & Silkies	2.5mm	2.5mm	12
Medium Woven	Poplin	4.0mm	3.0mm	12-14 (80 or 90)
	Gabardine	4.0mm	3.0mm	12-14
Medium Knit (Use stretch needle)	Jersey	4.0mm	2.0mm	12-14
	T-shirting	4.0mm	2.0mm	12-14
	Double Knit	4.0mm	2.0mm	12-14
Heavy	Denim	5.0mm	2.0mm	14-16 (90 or 100)
	Terry Cloth	5.0mm	2.0mm	14-16
	Corduroy	5.0mm	2.5mm	14-16
	Velour	5.0mm	2.5mm	14-16
	Wools	4.5mm	3.0mm	12-14

LOVE AND CARE OF YOUR SERGER

Keep It Clean

Lint quickly builds up under the throat plate and can clog knife blades, causing skipped stitches. If lint builds up on the thread guides, it can cause uneven threads feeding through the machine. Dust often with the soft brushes supplied with your machine or use a mini vacuum.

Oil as Necessary

Use an oil specially made for sergers. Check your manual for oiling points. Many machines need to be oiled after 8-10 hours of high speed serging. If your machine is making more noise than usual, it likely needs oil.

Change Needles

Needles with sharp, smooth points are essential to care-free serging. If the needle is slightly dull or burred, it will cause a clicking noise and possibly skipped stitches. Synthetic fibers dull needles more quickly than natural fibers. Change the needle when skipped or irregular stitches occur. Sometimes changing to a different **size** needle improves stitching quality.

Change the Knife Blades

If you avoid cutting pins, your knives last much longer. When the trimmed edge is ragged, however, one or both blades may be dull. One is made of hard alloy steel and rarely needs changing. The other is softer so is usually the only one that will be dull or damaged. Thick fabrics and synthetics also dull blades faster. Check your manual to see which of the blades on your serger is the softer one (it will be the least expensive). **Replace** a dull blade, being sure it is inserted properly.

NOTE: Serger knives cannot be resharpened like scissors with a "knife" edge. They cut because of the downward force of the two rectangular edges coming together.

CHAPTER 21
HELPFUL NOTIONS

Some of these notions come with your serger, but all of them can be purchased separately. Here's what they're used for:

Basting Tape
Regular and water-soluble basting tapes hold fabrics like slinky, silk-likes in place while serging.

Extension Table
Creates a flat surface around the serging area.

Glue Stick or a
Temporary Spray Adhesive
Holds slippery fabrics together for easier serging. Will wash out.

Lint Brush
Used to clean small areas.

Loop Turner or Tapestry Needle
Used to bury tails chains under your stitches.

Looper Threader
A wire with a hook at one end is used to pull thread through a looper.

Magnifying Lens
These attach to the front of your serger and magnify threading and stitching.

Melt-adhesive and Fusible Thread
Used in the lower looper, this thread is wrapped with fusible that melts when ironed to fuse the seam.

Needles, Needle Threaders and Inserters
Have lots of sizes available. The Perfect Needle Threader from Australia is also a needle inserter.

Screw Driver or Allen Wrench
These are used for changing needles and knives. Some will come with your serger.

Seam Ripper
Rip any serged seam quickly. Look for the new surgical types that easily slide under the looper threads.

Seam Sealant
Secure stitches with a liquid plastic like Fray Check® and Fray-No-More®.

Serger Knives
A replacement for the softer knife comes with your serger, or it can be purchased as can the more expensive steel alloy knife.

Serger Foot Pedal Mat
Slotted rubber mat prevents pedal from sliding.

Serger Stops
A pad that is placed under your serger to stop it from moving on the table top.

Thread Nets
Prevent slippery threads from dropping off the spool or cone while serging.

Thread Holders and Stands
These are used to hold extra spools or decorative threads on rods behind the serger.

Trim Catchers
This is a hand accessory that sits under your serger and has a bag to catch all of those messy clippings.

Vacuum Attachments
Mini adapters are available that attach to your normal vacuum hose. They have narrow tips to fit into small places.

CHAPTER 22

DIFFERENTIAL FEED

To understand the term "differential feed," you must first understand the term "feed dog." **Feed dogs** (or puppies, as Sue would say) are sets of metal "teeth" built into a sewing machine or serger below the presser foot. They grab fabric, move it along, then sink below the throat plate and move toward the front of the machine and up to begin again. There may be one or more sets, but all move at the same rate.

#1 for normal sewing. Space between feed dogs remains the same.

Front

Differential feed dogs are two sets of teeth, one in front of the other. The speed of the front feed dog is controlled by a dial or lever with numerical settings which might include 0.5, 0.7, 1 (sometimes N), 1.25, 1.5, 1.7 and 2.

PREVENT STRETCH IN SWEATER AND OTHER STRETCHY KNITS

With differential feed—Set the dial on number 2. This means the front feed dog moves twice as much fabric under the presser foot as the rear feed dog lets out, creating a gathering or "easing" effect. This prevents stretch.

#2 Space increases. Front speed increases.

Without differential feed—Push fabric into the presser foot with your fingers. Manufacturers use this trick to ease.

GATHER ON A SERGER

With differential feed—Set the dial on number 2. Use a lightweight fabric and the serger will actually gather it.

Without differential feed—Tighten your needle tension and use a long stitch length on lightweight fabrics. Gather can be adjusted by pulling up the needle thread after removing the fabric from the machine.

PREVENT PUCKERING

With differential feed—Set the dial on number 0.5 or 0.7. The front feed dog will move five or seven tenths as much fabric under the presser foot as the rear feed dog lets out, creating a "stretching" effect.

#0.7 Space decreases. Front speed decreases.

Without differential feed—Loosen the needle tension and hod the fabric taut if necessary. Both methods are helpful when serging a rolled edge in lightweight fabrics.

CHAPTER 23

SERGER FEET AND ACCESSORIES

Serging with your feet is an increasingly popular activity. More and more enthusiasts are looking for ways tot stretch the utilitarian and creative capabilities of their sergers, and have realized that having the right feet can make a difference. When purchasing a new serger, ask what feet are standard, what are optional, and if there are any other generic or branded feet that will fit. If you already own a serger, call your dealer occasionally for an update on what new feet are available. Once you've purchased a foot, experiment! Undoubtedly you'll devise new timesaving and creative uses in addition to those mentioned here.

Many of the new serger feet are snap-on. Don't worry if your model uses shank-style feet; your dealer probably has a snap-on adapter available. Also, not all the feet shown are compatible with all models, and although the finished technique may look the same, the configuration of the foot or attachment used will likely vary brand-to-brand, and possibly model-to-model.

Some cautions: Remember, only certain branded or generic feet are interchangeable among brands, and even then, may be limited to specific models. If in doubt about the suitability of a foot, buy it with a return guarantee, follow the instructions, and test-serge with care, removing any needle(s) that are not necessary, and turning the handwheel to advance the stitch.

Narrow Rolled Hem Foot

For narrow rolled or balanced finishing and/or finishing or seaming; the stitch is formed over the narrower, shorter stitch finger. Some new models do not require changing to a special foot for narrow serging. May require a special plate, also.

Transparent Chainstitch Foot

For serged chainstitching; the clear foot allows viewing the stitch as you serge. Also, handy for shirring, using elastic thread in the chainstitch looper.

serged chainstitch

Blindhem Foot

For serged blindhemming. Some are available in different sizes for different thicknesses of fabric. Also, works well for guiding the fabric when flatlocking, or for any time serging without trimming is desired.

guide-width adjustment screw

guide

Elastic/Taping Foot, Elastic Guide Foot

For regulating the amount of elastic stretch while it is being applied. Also, can be used for applying narrow ribbon or trims.

stretch adjustment screw

elastic

Cording or Gimp Foot

For precise serged application of cording or gimp. Different sizes may be available for different size cording or finer gimp. Also can be used to apply fine wire or fishing line.

cording

Lace-sewing Foot

For ultra-narrow seaming and finishing of lace and trim insertions, so popular for heirloom serging (pages 105-109).

edge guide

Piping Foot

For uniform, smooth insertion of piping in a serged seam. The piping is guided through a groove in the bottom of the foot. Also, for making piping trim. Sometimes called a "cording" foot.

groove

piping

Ribbon-sewing Foot

For "hands-free" serged application of narrow ribbon or trim. Some standard serger feet integrate ribbon application capability.

ribbon

Bias Tape Guide/Piping Foot

For creating and inserting piping in a serged seam. Also, for making piping trim.

flat bias strip

piping

piping filler cord

Bias Binder Attachment

For making and applying bias binding; the flat bias strip is folded around the edge, and secured with serged chainstitching.

Pearl/Sequin or Beading Foot

For easy, smooth application of bead strands. The strand is fed through channels under the back and over the front of the foot. Also works well for applying sequins, heavy wire, cording, and fishing line.

Shirring, Gathering, Ruffling Foot

For gathering of the lower layer while serging it to the flat top layer. Used in combination with differential feeding.

Fabric Separator Attachment

Also for gathering of the lower layer while serging to the flat top layer. Used in combination with differential feeding.

Gathering Plate

Like the fabric separator, for gathering of the lower layer while serging to the flat top layer. Also used in combination with differential feed.

Cloth Guide Attachment

For gauging even seam allowances and cutting even-width strips of fabric.

INDEX

Products from Palmer/Pletsch

Look for these easy-to-use, information-filled sewing books and videos in local book and fabric stores, or contact us for ordering information.

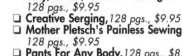

8½"x11" BOOKS:

- ❏ **Bridal Gowns,** *160 pgs.,$19.95*
- ❏ **The BUSINE$$ of Teaching Sewing** *128 pgs., $29.95*
- ❏ **Couture**—The Art of Fine Sewing *208 pgs., $29.95*
- ❏ **Creative Home Decorating Ideas** *160 pgs., $19.95*
- ❏ **Dream Sewing Spaces,***128 pgs., $19.95*
- ❏ **Fit For Real People,** *256 pgs., $24.95*
- ❏ **Looking Good,** *160 pgs., $19.95*
- ❏ **Pants For Real People,** *176 pgs., $24.95*
- ❏ **Sewing Ultrasuede® Brand Products** *128 pgs., $16.95*
- ❏ **Théâtre de la Mode,** *192 pgs., $29.95*

MY FIRST SEWING BOOK KITS *by Winky Cherry.* A series of learn-to-sew book kits for children ages 5 and up. Teacher materials also! Price per kit: *Hand Sewing Series: $14.95* *Machine Sewing Series: $12.95*

PerfectFUSE INTERFACING
Available in 1-yard and 3-yard packages:
- ❏ **PerfectFuse SHEER** *$7.95/$23.50*
- ❏ **PerfectFuse LIGHT** *$7.95/$23.50*
- ❏ **PerfectFuse MEDIUM** *$7.95/$23.50*
- ❏ **PerfectFuse TAILOR** *$8.95/$26.50*

- ❏ **Perfect WAISTBANDS** *1" x 5 yds: $4.00*

Videos are available in VHS only.

5½"x8½" BOOKS:

- ❏ **Easy, Easier, Easiest Tailoring** *128 pgs., $9.95*
- ❏ **Creative Serging,***128 pgs., $9.95*
- ❏ **Mother Pletsch's Painless Sewing** *128 pgs., $9.95*
- ❏ **Pants For Any Body,***128 pgs., $8.95*
- ❏ **Sewing With Sergers,***128 pgs., $9.95*
- ❏ **Sew To Success!,** *128 pgs., $10.95*
- ❏ **Smart Packing,** *240 pgs., $19.95*
- ❏ **The Shade Book** *144 pgs., $11.95*

DVDs — *$19.95 each*
- ❏ **Sergers Basics** (2 hr.)
- ❏ **Creative Serging** (2 hr.)

VIDEOS— *$19.95 each*
- ❏ **Creative Home Decorating Ideas** (1 hr.)
- ❏ **Creative Serging I** (1 hr.)
- ❏ **Creative Serging II** (1 hr.)
- ❏ **Perfect Fusing** (45 min.)
- ❏ **Sewing to Success** (45 min.)
- ❏ **Sergers Basics I** (1 hr.)
- ❏ **Sergers Basics II** (1 hr.)
- ❏ **Sewing With Ultrasuede** (1 hr.)
- ❏ **Time Saving Sewing** (45 min.)
- ❏ **2-Hour Trousers** (1 hr., 40 min.)

We also offer workshops and teacher training, **Perfect Sew Wash-Away Fabric Stabilizer, Perfect Pattern Paper,** *plus additional products for children and teachers.*

Palmer/Pletsch Publishing
1801 N.W. Upshur St, Ste 100 Portland, OR 9720
(503) 274-0687   ORDERS: 1-800-728-3784
www.palmerpletsch.com